The Little Blue Penguins of Wallaby Street

Dear Aidan,
Happy Investing!
Ashley J

Zoe J

Ashley Jarc and Michael Ashley
Illustrated by Zoe Jarc

Written by Ashley Jarc and Michael Ashley

Illustrated by Zoe Jarc

First published in the Unites States of America by Little Blue Penguin Finance, 2025

ISBN 979-8-218-87733-0

Little Blue Penguin of Wallaby Street

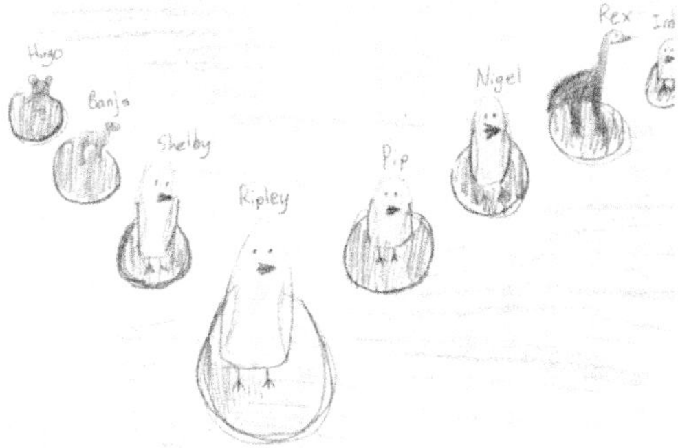

For Zoe and Leo

Preface

The inspiration for this book came to me many moons ago, shortly after the birth of my daughter. Around the same time, my son turned two. Between late-night diaper changes and early morning feedings, saving and planning for our kids' financial futures were front of mind. As my husband and I tracked our investments, I would often narrate our choices aloud for my kids, fully realizing that what I was detailing would be hard for their young brains to grasp. Nonetheless, I thought that by planting the seeds of financial language and know-how, I might inspire them to be more thoughtful about how they handled money, when the appropriate time came. We speak to our newborns in languages they don't know. Why not do the same with finance, I thought.

Then came the day I (sadly) realized that P/E multiples, stock tickers, and the YahooFinance app were unattractive to my kids, despite how addicting and interesting I find them. Given the choice among a glossy book, the

PBSKidsGames app, virtually any genre of music, and a finance app, the finance app never won out. Talking about money in abstract terms wasn't my little humans' jam, and it still isn't something everyone enjoys doing as adults.

I get it. Money topics can be tedious and stressful for some. Others might find them boring or inaccessible, especially if a finance resource reads like a textbook. But finance isn't boring to me at all, and I don't think it has to be. It's also extremely relevant, and money (like it or not) underlies the way each of us lives. The sooner we embrace discussions of money and personal finance, the better equipped our kids will be to make sound financial choices of their own.

My hope with this book is to inspire the next generation of kids to embrace their financial 'presents' and futures. Along the way, I hope to engage parents in the conversation, too. There are plenty of us who never had sufficient exposure to finance that could have helped us effectively manage our money. Many of us, including myself, wished we had known sooner what we know now. Let us teach our kids—all kids—basic concepts of personal finance and investing, so that they are prepared and empowered for their futures. Now.

In the pages that follow, I hope readers find themselves immersed in a story of adorable little blue penguins whose wise and timely financial choices change their lives. Adventure, friendship, overcoming adversity, earning, saving, and investing are core elements.

Next, let the story motivate us to start conversations about money at home. In our trusted circles, let's start talking about how and how much to save and where to invest. I would love these talks to happen across all ages and income levels, starting today. Finance and financial literacy have the power change lives, and, I argue, effectively to address income inequality. What could be more exciting and relevant?

DISCLAIMER: I am not a financial advisor or planner, nor do I seek to impart specific investment advice. There are many paths to financial success, and I aim to illuminate one such possibility. There is an element of luck and timing to investments, and that is also true for this tale. I might even argue that's the case for most good stories. But there are also certain principles, namely saving and investing strategically for the long-term, beginning at a young age, that I hope shine through. I do not encourage kids or their parents to stock-pick willy nilly or to put all their money into a single investment without proper planning, inquiry, or perhaps even advice.

I am keenly interested in broadening access to financial concepts and improving financial literacy across members of all income levels. Here's to starting and continuing conversations around money. Let's further help all kids (and perhaps their parents) take the first step on their personal finance journeys. For those of you fortunate to find yourselves along a solid path to financial success already, may this story serve as pure entertainment and supplement the conversations you're already having.

One final detail: The financial parameters surrounding the investment choices of this story are based on relatively high interest rates and a strong bull market.

Acknowledgments

I am forever indebted to my husband, Tony, and my curious, awe-inspiring kids, Leo and Zoe. You are the reason for this book. It was your unwavering support that helped me get this project started and completed. I couldn't have done it without you.

To my mom, thank you for the endless encouragement and for being available whenever I needed a second pair of eyes (or ears).

To my co-author, Michael Ashley, I extend a heartfelt thanks for the brainstorming, collaboration, and motivation. You removed the lonely solitude that often accompanies writing journeys of this magnitude and helped bring a touching story to life.

Holly Geerdes was an early supporter. Your friendship, counsel, and introductions have brought more joy than you can imagine.

I am grateful to Taylor Morris for her detailed, encouraging, and timely comments (and emojis).

In addition, I owe much appreciation to Stephanie Wildman-Tobriner, Brian Weisfeld, and countless other children's book authors connected to SCBWI who generously provided thoughtful input and advice.

To the friends and former colleagues who supported me, even when you didn't need to: Thank you. These people include but are not limited to Alexandra and Eddie Sarrine, Sanj Dutta, Andrea Villa, Andrew Matthieson, Beau Boren, Patrick Clingan, Erin Pittman, Ivory Blanchard, Katie and Wyatt Debski, and all the amazing teachers, staff, students, and parents at State Bridge Crossing Elementary School.

From the bottom of my heart, thank you, all.

Contents

1

Australia: Land of Joy/Misery

The land down under is supposed to be sunny. Cheery. *Happy*. Australia is the delightful outback where kangaroos bounce. It's the country (and continent) where cute, furry koalas munch on eucalyptus leaves. It's where brightly colored parrots flutter through tropical rainforests.

It's also where duck-billed platypuses...well, actually, what do duck-billed platypuses do anyway? What even *are* duck-billed platypuses?

Seriously, have you ever stopped to think about how intriguing duck-billed platypuses are? It's as though some crazy, mad scientist mashed a bunch of animals together and said, "OK, I took you this far. But I'm busy. Now you're on your own."

Duck-billed platypuses have the clawed hindfeet of a raccoon, the webbed forefeet of a goose, a tail that was clearly ripped off some poor beaver, and a bill shaped like, you guessed it, a duck's. And for some reason, biologists consider these blokes mammals—even though they lay eggs. Woah.

Sorry, where were we? Oh, yes. We were discussing how Australia is supposed to be such a joyful place, filled with amazing creatures and landscapes. You'd think any land that literally has ocean pools would just have to be fun.

Hold up. *What are ocean pools?* you may be asking. They're *almost* like residential swimming pools—but in the ocean. Seriously. This is a thing. Ocean pools or seawater pools—as they sometimes are also called—are located off rocky surf coasts. Protected from large, crashing ocean waves and whitewater, ocean pools make it possible for people like you and me to safely swim in saltwater. Now, just imagine you put a water slide into this ocean pool...

From afar, you'd think that any country boasting these luxurious ocean pools and duck-billed platypuses galore would be a wonderful, fantastic, happy place to live.

But you'd be wrong. *Dead* wrong.

This corner of Australia is no fun at all for little blue penguins. Not for one second.

Sidenote: If you thought those strange duck-billed platypuses were cute, little blue penguins will blow your mind. They're super cute. Really beyond cute. Like the kind of cute you observe in a baby panda who's eating a tiny ice cream cone while riding a toy tricycle. Then imagine if someone showed you a video of this same baby panda on YouTube. You'd scrunch up your own cute little face and go, "Ohmygoshthatssoinsanelycute!"

Unfortunately, cuteness only gets you so far in this life.

Especially in these parts of Australia. That's what ten-year-old little blue penguin Ripley has learned—the hard way.

"All I ever do is work," she thinks to herself daily. "The only thing my dad does, when he's not paralyzed by sadness, is work. The only thing my best friend Shelby and my brother Pip ever do is...work. In fact, all the other penguins in our sad little burrow-town do is work! Work. Work. Work."

Speaking of that word *work*, that's where Ripley is headed now. As in, at this very moment. Alongside a hundred other adorable little blue penguins in her community, she's off to work.

Why's this scene sad? In fact, it's painfully sad. Can you imagine working every day with no reward and no end in sight? It would be like nonstop homework, followed by chores—with no breaks, no TV, no treats, no playtime, and DEFINITELY no video games. Gasp!

But why must Ripley go to her job site? She's just a kid! you wonder. That's because work's truly the only thing she *can* do. A long time ago, that's what her ancestors agreed that her rookery of penguins would do. FOREVER. Every. Single. Day.

There will never be lounging in super cool ocean pools packed with twisty, turning water slides or green foam noodles for these poor penguins!

Nope. That's not at all how these little blue dudes and dudettes spend their days.

Every morning before the sun rises, you can see (well, you could, if you were a bird in the sky or a spectator from these hilltops) a big pack of little feathered *pingüinos*—that's Spanish for penguins—marching from their cozy burrows to the seashore. Do they look happy marching? What do you think? No, they do not. Let's rephrase things. *Marching* sounds too upbeat.

When you think of marching, you might imagine a drum line and some peppy music. That's *not* what we're talking about here.

In fact, we're going to replace all mentions of *marching* with *trudging*. No more *marching* in this story. The next time you reread this chapter (next week), or when your little human sister Zoe picks up this book and starts asking you a whole lot of questions about koalas and ocean pools, you stop in the middle of the conversation, and you say to her, "Look, Zoe. I love you. But these little blue penguins were *trudging* to the seashore."

Trudging really is the only way to describe this penguin progression. The word *trudging* puts a visual in your mind. Right? You can picture someone who's hanging his head, going somewhere he dreads. Each additional step he takes is harder than the last. Why? This verb lets you know that no matter how bad the current part of the story is, what comes next will most certainly be worse.

Much, much worse.

Imagine you didn't want to go somewhere. Maybe it's to the dentist's office because you've been told she needs to pull out your teeth. But you ask, *Why would a dentist pull out all my teeth?* Good question—yet again, smart readers. Maybe you ate way too much candy on Halloween. Imagine, in fact, that you ate bags and bags and bags of candy. After that, you ate your friend's candy when he wasn't looking. And then, you washed it down with a huge milkshake—after dumping in extra vanilla ice cream, chocolate syrup, and a bunch of candy bars for good measure.

That would be a LOT of sugar! And sugar, as you surely have heard, can cause cavities. It can also create bad breath and intense pain in your mouth. Your only remaining option after devouring so much sugar would be to go to the dentist, where you would have your teeth pulled out, one painful yank at a time—until they were...all gone.

Yikes!

You probably wouldn't walk too fast from the car to the dentist's office on that fateful day. No, you would walk slowly. Really slowly. You would *trudge* your way to the dentist, dreading what was in store for you.

This, dear readers, is how our little blue penguins start their morning. Every. Single. Day. They trudge down their grassy hillside to the shoreline, around a hundred of them. And they work. And work. And work.

But what if they don't want to work? What if they suddenly said "no" *to working?*

It's time to find out. (Here's a hint: They'd be in a lot of trouble.)

2

Catch Your Quota—Or Else

Can you believe *barfing* is a routine part of our little blue penguins' day? Just imagine if your future boss sat you down, on your very first day, and said to you, "Congratulations on getting this job. Now it's time to start barfing." You'd probably be a bit surprised, right?

But this *is* how our little blue penguins live. They barf up anchovies after catching them. That's how these penguins get the anchovies back to shore—to eat them (or turn them in).

In case you weren't aware, anchovies are salty, and they get even brinier (another word for saltier) when they're processed and canned. We're talking really salty. Like no-saliva-left-in-your-mouth salty. Don't believe us? Ask your parents to pack anchovies in your lunchbox someday, and try the morsels for yourself.

You'll be running for the drinking fountain in no time.

Sidenote: Some grown-ups really *love* to eat anchovies. Maybe it's the saline taste on their tongues, reminding them of the ocean, where anchovies originate. Or maybe some grown-ups just pretend to like them so they can look cool in front of their friends.

"Hey, look at me!" they might say between brackish bites. "I'm eating lots of smelly, little fish, and no one can stop me."

Either way, anchovies are a big deal down under.

How big? Let's just say Banjo, a dastardly dingo (also known as a mangy, wild dog)—who's just a despicable dude—and the archvillain of our story, grew very rich because of anchovies. Before Ripley was born, her great-great grandpenguins and their friends struck a deal with this scoundrel, Banjo. To find out what happened, let's transport you back in time.

Picture a family of three generic (is there such a thing?) little blue penguins. Wearing old-timey bonnets, a mama, a papa, and a baby penguin rest in their burrow. A fireplace glows in the corner. It's morning time. The mama penguin yawns as she wakes up. After stretching, she heads for the exit. "I'm going to catch us some breakfast," she sings to her sweet family. "See you soon."

But the second the mama penguin steps outside, she lets out a choking scream. "*EAREAREARGG!*"

With dread in his eyes, papa penguin looks at baby penguin. "I'll go see what's happened to her."

But again, the moment papa penguin steps outside, he too lets out a choking scream. "*EAREAREARGG!*"

Then baby penguin, more curious than scared, mutters, "What a scream! I wonder what that could be."

That last, fateful time that our naïve, vulnerable baby penguin goes outside, a gargantuan, flightless bird carries the screaming baby penguin off into the distance. The odd bird looks like an ostrich with wiggly red wattles (chin skin) and a bony, blue helmet on his head. Dead mama penguin. Dead papa penguin. And dying baby penguin.

"Anyway, that's what the legend teaches us, whippersnappers," says Indigo, a respected female penguin, whose blue feathers are streaked with gray. "Cassowaries are the absolute scariest beasts on earth, and they're only afraid of one slightly less but still extra-scary, savage barbarian—Banjo."

While she tells her story, Indigo instructs Ripley, Pip, Shelby, and an absent-minded penguin named Larry, on the latest fishing techniques. Each blue-feathered bird takes a turn diving for anchovies and barfing up what they have caught. (You don't read a sentence like that every day!)

Out at sea, the young penguins form a circle around Indigo, who shows them a new dive to use while they catch their quotas (required amounts). She then has them vomit the fish back into nets that Banjo's officers, the cruel seagulls, guard.

"I still don't think cassowaries are real," Pip squeaks out in between his dives.

As she hears this, Indigo almost chokes as she upchucks her anchovies. She fixes her gaze on Pip. Then Indigo pinches her wiry eyebrows together and leans toward him until her beak almost touches his. Staring directly at him, she speaks slowly.

"I assure you. Cassowaries are very real. The only thing standing between us and those flightless freaks, the cassowaries, is...*Banjo*." Ripley notices that the graying penguin lowers her voice to a barely audible whisper when she utters *his* name.

"If it weren't for *B's* protection," she says, pointing to the seagulls with nets, "you'd be dead where you stand. We all would. As much as we loath him, we need him, too. And he certainly won't protect us for free. So just keep fishing and puking."

Speaking of being dead where you stand, Ripley can't help noticing and then worrying about the daydreaming penguin. Though Pip, her brother, is two years younger than Larry, he's already caught three anchovies and barfed them into the net. Shelby has barfed up four himself—even after eating a few when no one was looking.

But Larry? What has he produced? Nothing. Nada. Zilch.

He doesn't even *pretend* to duck his little blue head under the waves like the others. No way is he going to catch thirteen anchovies for Banjo today if he keeps up this snail's pace. Normally, Ripley wouldn't care. She could easily catch more than her limit and spit a few extras to her fellow penguins. But not these last few months. She has had to save every extra catch hoping to cover her dad's quota, too.

Without her extra anchovies? Her dad, Nigel, would be as dead as that generic papa penguin from Indigo's legend.

"Hey, kid," Ripley says out of the side of her beak so the seagulls overhead won't notice. With dark, mirrored sunglasses covering their eyes, it's impossible to tell when or whom the seagulls are watching. "Hey, catch your quota. You know the drill," Ripley barks at Larry.

Larry acts like he can't hear her. He just floats on his belly, doing anything but work.

"I have a question." Pip turns to Indigo. "Why *does* Banjo need all of these anchovies anyway? We pay him for his protection, but why does he demand so much from us?"

Indigo winces at hearing the evil dingo master's name spoken so casually. She steals a glance at one particular seagull who's holding a net of anchovies several feet above them. "Your place is not to ask, Pip. Catch your quota. And be glad you're alive."

Sound advice.

Ripley heeds that same warning, splashing down under the waves and back to work. In seconds, she spies a school of anchovies treading water. "Sorry, fellas," she says to herself, as she often does before striking her small prey. Ripley feels sorry for the puny guys and how vulnerable they appear. But she has no real choice. Surprising herself, she nabs not one but two anchovies at once. Success!

Then she breaks the ocean's surface with glee, an anchovy tail peeking out of her full, smiling beak. Unfortunately, her satisfaction vanishes in an instant.

To her horror, she glimpses two seagulls flying off with Larry. Larry's pinched between their sharp talons. He screams and squirms to no avail. "No! Don't let them take meeee..." His voice trails off.

Ripley shudders. Then she notices that Indigo has also begun trembling. In fact, Ripley and Indigo are not alone. Up and down the coastline and floating on waves, countless little blue penguins watch helplessly as the seagulls loosen their grip and drop Larry at the feet of an oversized Tasmanian devil. This hairy monster's named Bork, and he's another of Banjo's evil helpers.

"Poor thing. But we tried to warn him," Indigo mutters as she turns away.

But not Ripley. She has to watch. For a moment, she even locks eyes with Larry. And then it happens. Bork, his exposed teeth glistening in the sun and his razor-sharp claws raised in the air, pounces upon the poor penguin. Screams fill the air. When the hairy, beastly (and now sweaty) devil stops moving, the only thing remaining of Larry is a small pile of fluffy, blue feathers.

Behind the blue, tattered mound is an ominous sign. Its letters are large and prominent, which make it impossible for Ripley to overlook, even from meters offshore. Ripley winces as she stares at it for the millionth time. It displays a picture of Banjo's contorted, smiling face and these unforgettable words: Catching Your Quota = Freedom.

"Back to work," Indigo commands Ripley and her young pupils with a shrug and a long, defeated sigh. She tries to distract the little birds from the horror they have just witnessed, but how can she?

3

Sometimes You Have to Risk It All

Everyone knows the beach is *the* best spot to barf up anchovies for lunch. It's da bomb. And it's our penguin trio's fave.

Right around noon, Ripley and her little blue penguin friends are stoked to waddle from the sea to upchuck the anchovies they've caught for themselves. Banjo can't touch these.

"Nope, you can't touch these," Shelby raps to himself. "Daaaa, nah, nah, nah."

Thank goodness our little blue penguins get to eat!

Is there anything sillier than watching a bunch of little blue penguins taking tiny little steps to the shoreline, then huddling together, vomiting whole fish, and eating their lunch? Probably not. Unless you happen to catch a baby panda giving a miniature monkey a bubble bath. Okay, that might be sillier. But we digress.

Back to our little blue penguins—this is the only time all day that they get to do something for themselves. It's their lunch break. Their version of a coffee break. Their *me time*. And how does it always start? With this charming sound: *Blargh!*

Yup, that's the sweet roar of a hundred penguins hurling in unison.

Oh, sure. Every now and then you'll hear a few other pukey noises like *blech*. Or *gack*. Maybe even *blarf*. (We like *glech*. It's got the subtle, delicate notes of a *blech* mixed in with a bit of *gack*.) If you ever have the opportunity to listen to a bunch of little blue penguins barfing anchovies into the sand at lunchtime, take it. It's *kind* of like going to the symphony but with undertones of guttural gagging rather than violin vibrations.

"I've been thinking," Ripley says, upchucking two silvery fish that land on the sand in front of her with a satisfying thud. "Why must we barf up anchovies first if we're going to eat them anyway? Doesn't it make more sense to eat them straight up?"

As he listens to Ripley, Shelby distractedly crosses his eyes to stare at a tiny fish tail poking out of his beak. "Stay in my belly," he mutters to the tail in a deep, cartoonish voice before bursting into loud belly laughs. Then he starts to choke but manages to swallow—hard. *Gulp.*

"Precisely!" Ripley exclaims. "You get me, Shel." Ripley nudges Shelby with her flipper, a proud smile across her face. "Keep our catch in our bellies. Let them stay there."

Pip stares at Ripley like she's just sprouted another head, maybe one made of string cheese. "It's called *puke picnic*, sis. First, we spew, then we eat. Everyone knows that. Those are the rules."

"Yeah." Shelby agrees with Pip, quick to change his mind. His anchovies hit the sand with a nice, meaty smack—a sound he's come to love. He tosses his grub back for proper chewing. "How can we have a puke picnic without the puking? It's practically a tradition."

"Yeah, that's the best part." Pip lets out a small burp as he licks the tips of his flipper and wipes the edges of his beak.

"However, I *do* enjoy the chewing, too." Shelby pops another fish in his mouth.

Ignoring them both, Ripley turns her attention to the other penguins scattered along the sand. Up and down the beach, she observes all the birds she's grown up with. Truly like family to her, she knows each one so well. They've been through a lot together, even before she lost her mom.

(It might seem insane for a young blue penguin to know over a hundred of anything, let alone well, but take our word for it. Ripley is socially gifted. If she were on Instagram or TikTok, she'd legit have 10M+ followers. Trust.)

Back to the penguins—there's Kai, a super-chill blue bird who rarely gets mad about anything. His head feathers are a little longer than everyone else's and swoop oh-so-cooly over his right eye.

"No worries, mate," is his catchphrase. Or sometimes he goes with, "No worries, bruh," without ruffling a feather—his own or anyone else's. In his adorable Aussie accent, he says this to all of his fellow penguins. Well, to everyone but Indigo.

Wise, fiercely observant, and stoic are characteristics that define our Indigo. She's been through a lot. As such, she's highly protective and well-versed in tough love. At her core, she's a softy, but her hardened exterior makes her hard to read. She doesn't put up with any form of disrespect, unless it comes from Banjo or his enforcers, whom she fears more than anything.

Then there's Perry, short for Periwinkle. He's the opposite of chill. He's tense, scared, ice-cold—and definitely not in any super cool "ice cold" way. If Perry had a signature phrase, it would be "Meep!" which is the sound he makes right before running away from anything mildly frightening. Like his own shadow.

Ripley eyes Cobalt next. Time seems to slow. If Taylor Swift woke up one day as a little blue penguin, she'd probably date Cobalt. We're 99 percent sure. After she got bored of being a superstar, of course. Cobalt's so edgy and so cool.

Ahhh. Swoon. Cobalt's a master of the Griddy, and he can mew better than anyone. (Sorry, Travis Kelce, but in the penguin world, you got nothin' on Cobalt. Super Bowl wins or not.)

Ripley keeps watching her fellow penguins and asking questions about anchovy digestion to distract from the nagging worry in her head. She doesn't want to think about her dad, but how can she not? So she goes back to her earlier question for Shelby: "Why *do* we upchuck before we eat?"

"Rip, stop trying to be so *different* all the time. Everyone knows the reason we barf first, eat later," Shelby pipes up with a twinkle in his eye.

She awaits Shelby's brilliant answer. So does Pip.

"Simple. The sand makes the anchovies taste better," Shelby continues.

Ripley chuckles. "It does not!"

"Sure it does." Shelby points to one of Pip's barfed-up anchovies, lying on the beach. One of its eyes points straight at the sun. If this small fish weren't already dead, it would, most certainly, be blind.

"Sand gives fish that garlicky taste, that little *je ne sais quoi*." Shelby giggles. He's entertained by the conversation but not concerned with the real answer Ripley seeks.

"Pip, are you going to eat yours? I'm still hungry here, especially with all this talk of sand and garlic." Shelby closes his eyes and inhales deeply, his beak inches from Pip's dead, smelly fish.

Ripley's stuck on her inquiry. "Do you even know what *je ne sais quoi* means, Shel? And no, sand doesn't make anchovies taste garlicky. I love you to pieces, but sometimes I just don't know where your mind is!"

"Who knows!" Shelby giggles, his eyes still fixed on the feast before him. "Oh, oh, sorry! I mean it makes them taste buttery. I get my flavors mixed up sometimes. But I know tasty food when I find it." With that, Shelby steals one of Pip's anchovies and tosses it in his mouth, like you and I might eat popcorn at a movie theater.

"Hey!" shouts Pip.

Ignoring Pip, Shelby peers at Ripley. "What's up with you anyway? You're acting more strangely than usual."

"Oh, nothing." Ripley responds, a little too fast. She doesn't want to let Pip and Shelby in on her private concern: what to do if her dad doesn't show up for head count.

Shelby remembers an earlier conversation with Ripley from that morning. "You're worried about your dad."

Pip's eyes go wide as saucers. "What's wrong with Dad?"

Ripley's eyes narrow as she stares directly at Shelby. He wasn't supposed to say anything. "Nothing, Pip. Dad's just sleeping in."

Anxiety is now etched all over Pip's little face, the exact thing Ripley had wanted to prevent.

"Shelby!" Ripley yelps at him with a glare. She leans over and hugs Pip from the side. Then she rubs his shoulder in reassurance.

"Why does Dad sleep in so much? No one else gets to. Banjo would freak if he knew Dad wasn't out here fishing with all of—"

Shelby and Ripley cover Pip's mouth with their flippers.

"Shh! Do you want to get Ripley or your dad in trouble?" Shelby looks around to see if anyone heard Pip over the sounds of collective barfing and anchovy-chomping. Thankfully, no one has.

Pip leans in closer to his sister. "Now I'm really worried."

Ripley shoots Shelby another look. "See what you did?"

Shelby just shrugs before stealing yet another anchovy from Pip's uneaten pile. "It was a matter of time."

"Hey!"

"I'm helping you," Shelby explains. "When you're worried, the last thing you guys want to do is eat. It's not good for your...*smack, slurp...*digesshon." Shelby slurs his words with a smirk.

"Di-ges-tion," Pip corrects him. "You eat all the time. *Especially* when you're worried." Pip's eyes are fixed on Shelby's.

"That's different. I eat my feelings." Shelby arches his back, his flipper feathers clasping together over his full, squishy tummy, the way he always does after a meal. He smiles sleepily.

None of this conversation has made Pip feel better. His little blue face betrays more worry. Ripley puts her flipper back on his shoulder. "It's OK, Pip. Nothing bad will happen. I promise."

"But what if Dad doesn't get to the shore in time for head count?"

Pip has just voiced Ripley's actual concern. "Don't worry. He will."

"But what if he doesn't?" Shelby perks up, finally remembering what's at stake and thinking through the possible consequences.

Ripley wheels around to face him. "You, too? I told you guys he's coming. Dad *always* shows up right before head count, even when he sleeps in."

"Right. Nothing to worry about, Pip!" Shelby steals one final fish from Pip.

"Hey!"

"Mmm. *Maintenant je sais!* Tastes garlicky."

***

With only twenty minutes left until head count, Ripley's insides feel twisted like a rope that's been stretched too tightly. If her skin wasn't covered by feathers, you could see that her face is now pale with apprehension. Ripley, Shelby, and Pip wade back into the water for their second daily round of fishing.

"He still hasn't shown up." Pip bobs up and down on the waves, treading water beside Ripley.

Ripley follows her brother's line of sight to the Tasmanian devils perched on the beach. Her dad is nowhere to be found. It's 12:40 p.m., and like clockwork, Banjo's henchmen have their clipboards ready to check who's at work.

Saving for her dad's anchovy quota had always been the easy part. She could catch as many fish as Cobalt and the other big penguins.

What couldn't she do? Pretend to be her dad.

Pip interrupts her thoughts. "The last time someone didn't show up for head count, the seagulls fed him to the crocs."

"No, they didn't." Shelby swims up to them. "They fed him to the *sharks*."

"That's *not* helping." Ripley glares at him.

She looks up to see three seagulls circling, watching overhead.

"What are we going to do?" Pip points to their burrows at the edge of the beach. "Dad's running out of time, and we have no way to reach him!"

Again, Ripley looks up at the seagulls, then back to the shore. One seagull stops winging to stare at her from behind his shiny, mirrored shades. The seagull tilts his head, and the sun's reflection blinds her like a laser beam.

Onyx. The most vicious of Banjo's birds. Only hours ago, he had delivered Larry to his death simply for not catching his daily quota. What would he do if he caught her dad skipping head count?

Shuddering at the thought, Ripley dives underwater and away from Onyx's glare. When she resurfaces, he's gone, interested in monitoring someone else.

Pip floats nearby. So does Shelby. Both look spooked.

"Your dad's running out of time."

"Ripley, we have to do something." Pip's voice breaks as his webbed feet wriggle faster in the water.

Staring at those feet, it hits her: There's a place the seagulls cannot detect her movements, one place where she can escape their constant monitoring.

"I've got it."

Pip turns to her. Shelby does, too.

She whispers her plan in their ears, finishing with these words: "The gulls can't see me underwater, not until I hit shore."

"No way," says Pip. "That's too risky."

Shelby is more forceful. "You saw what just happened to Larry, Rip. Don't be insane."

"We're good swimmers. All I need is a few minutes there and back before head count. If you two distract Bork and his pals, and maybe the seagulls, I'll be fine. I'm thinking one of you could pretend to be drowning. It could work. Pip, what do you say?"

"Why would I be drowning? I'm a penguin. I was *born* for the water."

"Then just cause a commotion. Wave your flippers like crazy or something. Just make it believable."

"This is totes cray cray." Shelby waves his flipper in Ripley's face. You know Shelby means business whenever he lets his flipper get involved in a conversation. Just last week he nearly poked out Pip's eye in a quarrel over the best place to relieve himself at nighttime. (If you're wondering, he argued for the front of his neighbor's burrow. Pip fought for the bushes.)

Sorry for the defecating detour. Both Shelby and Pip shake their heads at Ripley and let her have it.

"Nope."

"Don't do it."

"It's bananas to do it."

"It's mad as a cut snake."

"You *can't* do it."

"*No one* can do it."

"Please. *Please* don't do it."

"Don't be a drongo!" (For those who don't speak Aussie English on the regular, drongo is another word for fool.)

This last appeal comes from Pip. His frightened little eyes stare right into his sister's, begging her not to swim to shore. Her chances of saving her dad are so low.

"It's too risky. Way too risky."

When Ripley replies, her voice has a far-away tone that Pip and Shelby instantly recognize. It's how she sounds when talking about the saddest part of her life. "Mom told me something once when I was little..."

Eager to know anything about their mom, Pip leans forward.

"Be the...Oh, never mind. I don't have time to explain. Just...sometimes you must do the very thing everyone else is too afraid to do."

"No!"

"Nooooo—"

But before they can stop her, Ripley has dived underwater. She propels herself forward, using her webbed feet and flippers as a powerful motor. Darting back and forth among her fellow penguins like a downhill skier, she zooms to the shoreline. She resembles a rocket more than an animal.

Halfway to shore, Indigo spots her.

Ripley panics. *Oh, no. She's going to try to stop me. She'll slow me down, try to make me turn back.*

Clever girl that she is, Ripley drags her flippers across the ocean floor, kicking up sand and shells in her wake. It's enough to temporarily blind Indigo.

"What in the blazes?!" Indigo screams in a warbled, underwater voice.

Of course, Ripley can't stop to explain. She has no time and almost no breath left. She'll apologize later. With one final push, Ripley torpedoes to shore.

The only thought in her perfect little blue head is this: *You got this, Pip and Shelby. Distract those Tasmanian devils. Those seagulls. All we need is two more seconds, once I hit land...*

Splash! (More like *reverse splash,* but what would you call that?)

Ripley's body shoots out of the water, feathers slicked back. As soon as her flat, adorable feet hit the sand, she starts pounding toward her burrow. She hustles, taking short, shallow breaths to remain undetected.

Behind her in the water, she hears Shelby's and Pip's loud shrieks as they continue to distract the Tasmanian devils, luring them to the water's edge. *I knew you could do it, Pip and Shel. Best mates a girl could ask for. I owe you guys.* A smile crosses Ripley's face.

Unlike the penguins they guard, Banjo's hairy henchmen sink like stones in the water. If they took one step closer toward Pip and Shelby, the waves would swallow the ghastly devils.

Then, out of the corner of her eye, to her horror, Ripley senses something else, something new.

A large shadow appears like a dark monster upon the sand. *It must be a bird*, she thinks. *Seagulls. Onyx. Oh, no!* But she doesn't have a chance to look up.

But why is this shadow so big? He must be flying high, close to the sun. That's why Onyx is blocking so much of the sun's light, she thinks. But still, he's sure to close in on her in seconds. Ripley's seen him do it countless times before.

She panics. Suddenly, she feels like she can't catch her breath. She starts to see stars.

Just a few more feet, she tells herself. *Be brave*.

Intense heat, as if from a fire-breathing dragon, beats down on her neck. Panting faster than ever, Ripley leaps behind a boulder.

She clutches her head between her legs and tries not to move. She holds her breath. Then she notices that she hasn't felt any pecking. She hears no seagulls screeching. *She panicked needlessly*, she thinks. Then Ripley cautiously opens her eyes.

But the heavy darkness overhead remains. Maybe it's a cloud, or perhaps she's become needlessly afraid of her own shadow. She thinks of Perry's paranoia and almost laughs with relief.

Ripley peers over her shoulder, one last time, before making her final dash to her burrow. She must prove that the shadow is, in fact, nothing to fear.

But it's not a cloud. It's not her shadow. It's not Onyx. It's not even flying.

"What the?!?" she gasps.

Fear cripples Ripley. Flash frozen, she stands as still as an iceberg. Above her towers a bird so enormous, so gargantuan it blocks the sky itself. It lowers its hooked beak toward her, ready to swallow her whole. As it does, she pees a little.

This is not anything she's seen before. This creature is stunning and colorful, like a peacock flying out of a double rainbow. It has a bony crest and legs that tower over her like bamboo shoots. She notices thick, sopping eye lashes and a neon-blue neck. Two long, loose, red pieces of skin dangle from its chin.

Oh, it can't be. Ripley hadn't planned for this. But this colossal, multicolored beast on stilts must be.

4

Running Out of Time

Giant doesn't begin to describe the size of the terrifying bird in front of Ripley. Its body is mostly covered in black feathers. It's an actual bird. A humongous bird. But it doesn't look like it can fly. Or can it? The creature towering above Ripley more closely resembles an ostrich.

A mutant ostrich? No.

A blood-thirsty dinosaur? No.

A dragon? Yessss. A fire-breathing dragon—mixed with a prehistoric dinosaur—who wears a Roman soldier's helmet. It has enormous eyes accented by full glam makeup.

And did we mention its claws? They might be actual daggers.

Yes! There. That's a more accurate description of the predator who's about to shred Ripley to pieces.

So, this is a cassowary, Ripley thinks in muted horror. An actual cassowary. Every blue penguin's worst nightmare. The bogeyman that little blue chicks ask their parents to check for at night.

All those scary tales Indigo had told them weren't pretend!

They were real. Really real. Like in-your-face real.

Ripley still tries to scream, but she can't. She's so petrified that no sound escapes her throat. Her beak is wide open and bone dry. She's pretty sure time has officially stopped. Her flippers extend straight at her sides. She can't blink. Imagine a piece of fossilized wood, and that's basically Ripley.

The creature's one shiny eye peers at her. Then the other does. Together they blink. Fast.

Next, the beast tilts its head hecka fast to the right and lunges toward Ripley. Sudden motion and the immediate threat of death free Ripley from paralysis. She gasps, squeezing her eyes shut, and holds up a flipper to protect herself—

But nothing happens. *Is she already dead?*

Ripley peeks through one eye.

"Augh!"

The cassowary's beak is still a mere inch from her face. And it smells like bat guano. Springing to her feet, Ripley slips between the beast's tall legs and bolts for home. She feels like she might throw up—out of fear AND from the awful smell—but she knows there's no time to stop.

In her panic, she doesn't notice Onyx the seagull circling overhead. He's careful not to let Ripley see his shadow. He watches intently to see which little burrow Ripley enters. Then he pivots to fly away but pauses. *Why was she so frantic?* he wonders. He can't help but watch her through the tiny window of her burrow.

***

"Dad? Dad?" pants Ripley, out of breath. "Where are you?"

She runs around their little nest, looking under his twig bed and between branches. Her father's nowhere to be found, making Ripley's little blue penguin heart pound even faster. What if the cassowary had come here first? *What if he had eaten Dad while I was at work?* What if that's why he hadn't shown up for head count?

That would mean she had lost her mom *and* her dad.

Heartbroken and exhausted, she collapses onto the ground, flipper over her eyes. She starts to cry but stops herself. Who would take care of little brother Pip if she fell to pieces?

For Pip's sake, I must keep it together. But then a new worrying thought hits Ripley.

"Oh, no! What if..."

She rushes over to the hammock where she sleeps at night. Directly below it, she finds the "X" that marks her secret trove. Sand flies passed her as her little flippers dig beneath the sand at a dizzying speed. Some of the sand gets flung through the window and catches Onyx's attention again. But he remains at a distance.

"Thank heavens!"

Ripley breathes relief as she feasts her eyes on her stash: A hundred and fifty perfectly preserved anchovies, each one meticulously preserved in a banana leaf. *Her life's savings.*

"G'day, sweetie. How's it going?"

Ripley startles as she hears her dad, Nigel, come through the back of their burrow. He carries little pink stones that weigh him down. Ripley quickly reburies her pile of anchovies under the sand behind her.

Her dad promptly drops what he's been holding to the ground. For the moment, Ripley forgets all about secret anchovies and the killer cassowary to marvel at the dozens of small crystals in front of her.

"What in the world are those?"

"Woolamai granite stones," Nigel says proudly, as if he had just discovered gold inside his belly button.

"Woolamai *what*?"

"Woolamai granite. Sourced right from our island."

"Just now?"

"Well, yes."

Ripley stares at the gems. They are incredibly beautiful. "But shouldn't you be at work—with us?"

"Your mother used to love these. They're almost as gorgeous as she is." Nigel rubs one of the beads between his flipper feathers, polishing it. "I want to make her a necklace—to remind her of how much she means to us. Don't you think she'll like it?"

Ripley smiles sweetly. She doesn't have the heart to remind her dad that her mom won't be coming back. She can't. Feigning courage, Ripley whispers to her dad, "I'm sure she'd love it."

Ripley thinks back to that dreadful day when Banjo announced he had taken her mom's life. No child should have to witness such horror or experience such pain. She feels a deep and familiar ache in her stomach. Then she shakes her head abruptly and squints to push the nightmare from her mind. She needs to stay focused.

Ripley repeats herself. "Dad, you were supposed to be at work. I had to cover for you. Again! We need to go."

Ripley also recalls the scary cassowary she just encountered. "Dad, you'll never believe what I just saw—"

He cuts her off. "But if I don't collect enough of these granite pieces, your mom won't get her necklace." Ripley realizes her dad isn't listening to her.

"*Won't get her necklace*? Dad, Mom's...*gone*." Ripley realizes she has been a bit harsh when she sees her dad slump down on the hammock, his feet floating above the floor, right above her stash.

She takes a deep breath and sits down beside him. Grasping his flipper in hers, she whispers. "Dad, Banjo took Mom away, remember? She's gone. Gone forever."

Nigel looks sadly at Ripley then hides his face from her view.

"I know, Ripster." A tear falls from his motionless head onto the sand below. "I just miss her so much."

Some days, her dad's so depressed he can't even get out of bed. *At least he was up and about today*, Ripley thinks.

Nigel stares at the stones scattered across the floor for a long moment. Then he perks up. "So, do you think Mom will like these?"

Ripley tugs her dad's arm. "Dad! Come on. We have to go. *Now*. Banjo's seagulls and the Tasmanian devils are going to start head count any second. If we're not there..." Ripley stops herself. She doesn't even want to think about what might happen to her dad.

Nigel reads her thoughts. "Oh, Banjo won't do anything to *me*. He respects me. Besides, he knows what a good diver I am. Did I ever tell you the story of how I caught twenty anchovies—in one hour? I have a reputation!"

Ripley sighs sweetly. "Only about ten thousand times. I know you're awesome, but we're running out of—"

Trying to cheer her up, he continues. "OK, Miss Smarty Pants. But did you know I had a head cold that day, and yet I still managed to catch all those anchovies? In one hour, mind you."

"Yes. Yes. You told Pip and me all about it—"

"But did you know my nose was stuffed up the whole time?"

"No, I didn't know that part. But we really must leave now—"

"Actually. My nose was *running* that whole day. Like a faucet."

"Fine. Fine. It was a faucet."

"More like a snot faucet. Just dripping down my nose. All day long."

"Snot faucet. Got it. Now, we really must go—"

"Maybe it was more like a booger faucet, now that I think about it. Are booger faucets a thing? Boogers don't really flow, though, right? They stick and get clumpy, right? Anyway, I really did have a lot of boogers that day. Both nostrils were totally packed—"

"DAD! I'm going to be sick. Banjo's not going to spare you this time if you don't show up for head count. The seagulls already killed someone."

"Really? But I'm a *legend*. I've caught more anchovies for Banjo than any other blue penguin in history."

So what? she wants to say. That was years ago. But she stops herself. "Look. It's nice that you used to be such a good diver, but Banjo doesn't care about your shared history. All he cares about is getting his anchovies. That's it."

Nigel's face changes as this realization dawns on him. "You're right. You think there's still time for me to catch my quota? I'm really fast, you know?"

Ripley smiles as she leads him out the door. "No need. I did it for you."

"You *did*?"

"Yep."

"Thank you, Ripster. How can I ever repay you?" He pats the top of her head with his flipper. "If only we didn't have to work this hard," he mutters, more to himself than to her. Ripley is tempted to tell him about the anchovies she has hidden in their burrow, but she stops herself.

Would he be mad at her for keeping a secret?

***

The moment father and daughter leave their den, Onyx swoops down. Remembering what he just witnessed, he eyes the lose pile of sand and starts digging.

5

Punishment—Banjo-Style

"Line up. Link up." Banjo's voice booms across the beach for head count.

When the little penguins hear the fearsome dingo speak, it makes their blue feathers stand on end, as if they have goose bumps. Wait a tick. That's silly. Little blue penguins don't get goose bumps, do they? If anything, they should probably get penguin bumps. No, that doesn't sound right either. We'll think about this and get back to you.

Anyway, back to the beach.

At this very moment, all the little blue penguins lock flippers, standing upright at attention, like tiny toy soldiers waiting for inspection by their commanding officer. Only this officer isn't a good guy. Nor is he an officer. He's Banjo the Bad, the scariest, snarliest, meanest dingo in all of Australia. New Zealand, too. He's pretty much the worst bloke in the whole southern hemisphere.

Also, this lineup doesn't contain all the little blue penguins. Two are missing. Can you guess which two? If you said Shelby and Pip, you haven't been following this story closely. But if you picked Cobalt and Indigo, you certainly *have been* following. Right on. Good job remembering their names! They're secondary characters after all.

But still, no. That wouldn't make much sense either.

Of course, the missing penguins are none other than father and daughter, Nigel and Ripley. The duo quickly rushes to join their fellow penguins, hoping to squeeze in place before Banjo can detect that they have been out of line. But Banjo misses nothing.

Nothing.

"Hold up. Something's wrong." He scans the beach with his mustard-yellow eyes. Banjo raises his right paw in front of him like a soldier with a bayonet, ready to fire at his enemies. His nose sniffs the air—once, twice...a third time.

No one besides Banjo moves an inch. Not even the Tasmanian devils who stand guard on either side of the little penguins. Banjo's seagull army, now gathered on the sand, stays perfectly motionless, waiting for his next command.

Guess who else doesn't move? Definitely not the rest of little blue penguins. They don't even blink. They don't breathe. They don't shudder either—although they'd sure like to. The sheer terror makes their adorable little blue tummies queasy.

Banjo struts up and down the penguin line, counting who is present.

When he reaches Pip and Shelby, they are so frightened they can barely hold it together.

"Achoo!" Pip sneezes.

"Bless you." The words escape Shelby's mouth before he can stop them.

Banjo towers over Pip who can no longer control his quivering body.

"Stop that," Banjo hisses.

Pip stops trembling. But that just makes him sneeze. Again.

"Bless you," says Shelby. Again.

Banjo turns to Shelby. Shelby cowers, covering his head with his flipper.

Banjo turns to Pip, but his jitters are all-consuming. Pip shakes like a maraca in a samba band.

"I said: *Stop tha*t!"

Pip finally freezes. Banjo pauses, expecting him to sneeze again. Instead, Pip toots. *Squeak!* The sound escapes his rump like a tiny mouse playing a teenier trumpet.

"Bless you," says Shelby. Again.

Enraged, Banjo lifts Shelby high off the ground by the scruff of his neck. He's about to chuck the young little penguin into the sea when—

"Look what I found."

Still gripping Shelby in his mangy paws, Banjo turns to see Onyx, winging through the air. In his talons, Onyx holds Ripley and Nigel. They squirm, attempting to free their necks from the seagull's tight, pinching clutch.

"I knew something was off." Refocused on his initial pursuits, Banjo flings Shelby into the air and out of sight. Though this movement requires little of Banjo's strength, Shelby soars so high that for a brief moment, he disappears above a cloud. Then he barrels back to earth and smacks the ground. *Kersquish.*

Banjo licks his lips with satisfaction, looking now exclusively at Ripley and Nigel. An evil grin spreads across on his face. Finding fun ways to punish penguins, especially when he has an excuse to do it, is his jam. "Bring those two to me."

Onyx releases his clutches, causing Ripley and Nigel to fall several feet to the ground. They land with another two thuds before the evil master. *Kersquish. Kersquish.*

Banjo delights in the fear he sees in Nigel's eyes. "So, it's *you*, old man. I never thought I would have to make an example out of you."

"No!" Ripley throws herself between Banjo and her dad. "It was *my* fault we were late. I was gathering...uh, Woolamai granite pieces. For a necklace! For my mom." Her voice dies on that last word.

Banjo scoffs. His head swivels toward her with fierce aggression. "*Your mom*? The ultimate traitor?"

"She was not a traitor," Ripley whispers.

Gasps arise from the terrified penguins. Little Pip sneezes again. And toots. Pip is mortified. Under his blue facial feathers, his cheeks glow red. (But, of course, you can't see that.)

"Bless you," says Shelby.

Banjo struts over to Shelby's new location. Without even looking, he backhands Ripley's friend so hard that Shelby slams into a nearby tree.

Banjo turns again to Onyx. "Where did you find these two turncoats?"

"I caught them at home. Eating anchovies. Your anchovies." Onyx can't resist the chance to suck up to his boss.

More gasps from the penguins.

"That's a lie!" says Ripley.

"Hush," whispers Nigel, as he grabs Ripley's flipper and squeezes it tightly but so no one can notice.

Banjo stalks around the father-daughter pair as he thinks. "Taking *my* anchovies is a serious offense, Onyx. Very serious. Can you prove it?" Banjo speaks louder than usual so that all onlookers are sure to notice.

"Indeed, I can."

Ripley's stomach churns. She swallows but almost chokes on her spit. Then her mouth goes dry. *The seagull must be lying*, she thinks. But she fears what's coming. Onyx is not only cruel. He's the cleverest of Banjo's baddies.

Onyx approaches his master with a deep bow. "Your orders clearly state that little blue penguins owe you all their anchovies." He motions to a chiseled stone in the distance that has lots of fine print etched on it.

"Correct. If these little blue half-wits expect me to protect them from ferocious cassowaries who, as we all know, could and would easily swallow them in one gulp, then they must abide by my rules: All anchovies are to be turned over to me. Besides the few I graciously allow them to eat. No exceptions."

"That's my understanding, too, Great One," agrees Onyx. "That's why it pained me so much to discover *this* today." Onyx disappears into the bushes but returns in a flash. What Ripley sees next nearly causes her to faint.

In his talons, Onyx holds Ripley's entire collection of a hundred and fifty anchovies, each of which is still carefully wrapped in a banana leaf. The other little blue penguins can't believe their eyes, especially Nigel whose little blue jaw is basically on the floor. Cries of "Oh, no!" and "Impossible!" spill out from the crowd in disbelief.

The only one who remains calm is Banjo, as if the blood in his body had just turned to ice. He pivots to Nigel and inhales deeply. "I should have known my best diver would one day betray me."

"No—" shrieks Ripley.

But Nigel cuts his daughter off with a raised flipper.

Banjo snatches Nigel by the shoulders. Banjo's wolfish features contort into a terrible toothy smirk. "I should have known. There's something rotten about your family that leads you to make stupid choices. First your wife. Now you." His low voice drips with menace.

"But—" Ripley tries to interject again.

Banjo beams his yellow eyes at Ripley, shutting her up. Then he refocuses on Nigel.

"Your wife lost her life because of betrayal. Apparently, you didn't get the message..."

Ripley sees her dad start to tremble. Nigel tries to control his tremors, but he can't. He shakes uncontrollably, fearing what's coming next.

"What am I to do with you, old geezer?" Banjo goes on. "Sending you away won't cut it. Sure, you'd eventually die, but that's too easy. I could kill you now. And painfully." He strums his toes against the sand as he thinks.

"Do it, boss!" shouts Bork who, to everyone's surprise, is the owner of a high-pitched voice. He's the same burly Tasmanian devil who shredded Larry earlier this morning.

"Torturous death *is* an option." Banjo tightens his grip on Nigel's shoulders, tearing feathers out with his strong paws. "But if I kill Nigel today, you little blue penguins might forget about him tomorrow. You would just go back to your selfish, rule-breaking ways. And the next thing I know, another one of you pathetic, flightless nincompoops would try to betray me."

Banjo spins around and scans the line of little blue penguins. He pauses and relaxes his expression. In a calmer, kinder voice he continues. "Anyone of you could be next—stealing my anchovies...and, and breaking years of mutual trust and adoration. We can't have that now. Can we?"

He pushes out his bottom lip as if to pout. His voice sounds gentle, like he cares about the penguins' well-being as much as his own. Then he pauses and straightens his posture. A bright Cheshire cat–like smile draws across his face.

"I know!" he declares with excitement. "What we need is a *permanent sign*. Something to remind you of my generosity and kindness. Of my...why yes, to remind you of my love."

Banjo rubs his chin. Then he snaps his fingers. "Onyx. Fetch me that."

Onyx looks in the direction that Banjo's pointing. Under a bottlebrush tree lies Shelby, passed out from the time Banjo flung him. Onyx flutters over, grabs Shelby, and deposits him at Banjo's feet.

Shelby wakes up. "Is it lunchtime?"

Banjo kicks Shelby.

"Buuughhh." Shelby clutches his stomach, wishing he hadn't come to.

"No, Onyx. I didn't mean bring me that annoying little penguin. I meant bring me some hot coal, from over there."

"Um..." Onyx looks around sheepishly. "You want me to bring you *hot coal*?"

Banjo rolls his eyes. "Did I stutter?"

Onyx bows deeply to his master. "Oh, Great One. Your every wish is my command. But I am not sure how I can bring hot coal. I mean for that I would need coal. And a fire maybe. I don't have either of those—"

"Ugh. Why is this so difficult? Bork." Banjo claps his paws rapidly, with growing impatience. "Bring me something hot. Very hot! Anything. At once!"

Bork is equally confused. "Boss? You want a coffee? But you just had one."

"Twits. I am surrounded by idiots." Banjo takes a deep breath. "Bork." He exhales slowly like he's holding a yoga pose. "Bring me something hot that can inflict pain. You can do *that*, can't you?"

"Right away, boss."

With that, the Tasmanian devil remembers a rusted bottle cap he had seen earlier that day. Next he whirls around like a spinning dervish. He creates a tornado of sand and smoke. For a moment, the entire beach is covered in a mini-hurricane of activity.

Seconds later, the once-intact bottle cap appears bent in half and glows a deep orange. Bork tosses it at Banjo's feet.

"Now for the easy part," says Banjo, his voice still ice cold. "With this gorgeous tool, I will create a friendly reminder of what happens when you cross your beloved Banjo."

Banjo drags the sharp, red-hot metal along Nigel's left shoulder. Nigel's body contorts under the pain, but Banjo has him clenched tightly.

"Baahhhhh!" Nigel shouts out with more force than anyone in the penguin colony has ever heard. "What did you do to me?"

As Banjo releases Nigel, he falls to the ground, grabbing his raw, now featherless shoulder, in utter agony. After a few seconds, Nigel and the rest of the onlookers peer down at the damage. Blood drips in streaks like crimson rain on a window.

Banjo motions scare quotes with his toes as he whispers the word adorable. "That should do the trick. You look lovely, Nigel, and you surely won't forget today's events. How I do admire my handiwork. I must say..."

"What's the 'T' for?" Nigel pants. He can somewhat make out the letter through blood and burned skin.

Ripley and the other penguins listen intently as Banjo, flanked by Onyx and the other henchmen, explains.

"'T' stands for traitor." Spittle flies from Banjo's mouth as he enunciates each syllable with intensity. "May my artistic masterpiece be a reminder to all of you ungrateful..." He pauses. "Pigeons."

Banjo has just hurled the ultimate insult at these penguins. "Yes, indeed, that's what you truly are...nothing but common pigeons. Do NOT cross me again, lest you desire a branding of your own."

Without her noticing, tears have welled up in Ripley's eyes. Inside, she curses herself for the terrible mess she's caused. This scenario is the exact opposite of what she had hoped. Not only do the other little blue penguins think her dad's disloyal, the kind of selfish penguin who would skip work to make jewelry and gorge himself on anchovies while his mates struggled—now he's been tortured and publicly humiliated. He's lost all dignity. How can he ever recover?

She wants to tell her dad she's sorry about everything, most importantly the savings. She never meant for any of this to happen. She only wanted to help him, to take care of her family so they didn't have to work so hard. But instead, she's made things worse.

Much, much worse.

"There, there," says Banjo to Nigel who can't stop staring as his wound, his mouth still agape. "It's not that bad. Think of it this way. You got a free tattoo today. Some animals would pay good money for such artwork." Banjo slaps Nigel hard on his uninjured shoulder.

"Just don't let there be a next time. Which reminds me, best get back to work and catch me my anchovies." Banjo points to the ocean.

Nigel waddles obediently into the water, anticipating just how badly the saltwater will sting his open sore.

Banjo smiles cruelly down at Ripley. She thinks she'll be sick.

6

In the Shade of the Magnolia Tree

Little blue penguins don't run fast. They can't. After all, they don't have knees.

Have you ever tried running with your legs completely straight? If not, give it a go. Then please tell us how it affected your ability to sprint during tag or your next game of hide-and-go-seek.

As a result of their physiques and genetics, penguins waddle. We're sure you've noticed.

Super swimmers that they are, they can jet around the ocean. They practically fly underwater. They also love diving in streamline to retrieve anchovies at very impressive speeds. Under the sea, these guys are in their element.

But on land?

They're usually kind of awkward. Like maybe even super awkward. Picture a three-year-old toddler on a sugar rush, trying not to bump into walls after having inhaled three big slices of birthday cake—washed down with a Big Gulp—and you'll have a good idea of how clumsy most little blue penguins appear on land.

Despite all that, Ripley is managing to run.

She bolts away from the terrible ordeal at head count and straight to her happy place, her secret hideout, her calm-down corner. Of course, she's not currently happy, but she hopes that when she arrives she will *become* happy.

Ripley's happy place sits under her favorite magnolia tree. The tree stands atop a secluded, grassy hill that overlooks the ocean, a good journey from the burrows. For those of you who haven't had the chance to curl up at the base of a magnificent magnolia tree, when it's in bloom, you haven't lived. On second thought, that might be too strong of a statement. But, seriously, check it out sometime.

What we mean is magnolia trees are magnificent. They're gorgeous. They're breathtaking. Their beauty can be a real pick me up when you're down in the dumps.

Known the world over for their large, waxy evergreen leaves and their showy, white, softball-sized flowers, magnolias are also some of the oldest trees on earth. Some tree experts think magnolias go all the way back—like way, way back—before humans even kept historical records.

As luck would have it, Ripley's magnolia is both old and splendid, too. It boasts five huge, gnarled trunks that split apart near the base like spoons bent in half. Ever since she was young, Ripley has loved to lie against its sturdy trunk or climb the tree's broad branches. Ripley imagines the branches are wrapping her in a huge hug. And it soothes her to look up at all those elegant white flowers, nestled among dark leaves.

Most of all, she loves listening to the birds who call this tree home. Ripley delights in their songs and the sounds their wings make when they fly. These are the rustlings and noises of New Holland honeyeaters and superb fairywrens (two native Australian bird species with incredible names). She takes comfort in the cackles of the cockatoos and gets stoked to hear the laughter of a kookaburra.

When things get tough for Ripley, the magnolia tree is a spot for her to escape. And let's face it: Things *have* been tough on Ripley. Even before today.

Rushing toward her magnolia, she tosses herself at its shaded roots. Huffing and puffing, her heart pounding, she leans back against the thick bark. It easily supports her weight, reassuring her that things will be OK.

But will they? she wonders.

If she were Pip's age, life would be so easy. She wouldn't fully understand how bad things were under Banjo. She could live a carefree life. Most of all, no one would tease her if she did cry over her problems. Some older penguin, like Indigo, might even lay a flipper on her shoulder when she was sad and say, "There, there," making everything better.

But not when you're ten.

Ripley thinks she's supposed to be mature, which is why she's slightly embarrassed to be so sad. But crying is *all* Ripley wants to do now. More than anything, she'd like a good old-fashioned cry-fest. Can you blame her?

After all that crying, Ripley knows she will feel much better.

Following a shockingly brief moment of sorrow, a new thought occurs to her. No way will she let mean old Banjo, his sidekick Onyx, or Bork—any of Banjo's crew for that matter—steal her mojo. Nope. Not happening.

I won't let them get to me, Ripley tells herself.

Lying back against the magnolia's strong trunk, the tree starts working its magic. Ripley thinks. She takes deep, slow breaths. Then she's reminded of a day from years ago and smiles to herself. She closes her eyes. In her mind, she envisions her late mom, Sapphire.

In her dream-like state, Ripley sits cross-legged in the shade of this same magnolia. Sapphire holds Ripley close. She rocks her slowly. Above them, an orange fireball of a sun dips behind the hills, casting its final rays before closing out the day.

Bathed in the hazy glow, Sapphire beams at her daughter. "Life can't always be perfect," she says softly. "But you are strong. You can handle more than you know." Sapphire's words both comfort and confuse Ripley at first.

In her vision, Ripley has been crying. She had just gotten her first bee sting—smackdab in the middle of her webbed foot. And, boy, did it hurt terribly. Tears stream down her face.

"I know you're in pain now." Sapphire squeezes her daughter and ruffles her blue head feathers. "But I'm going to clue you in on a secret."

Little Ripley looks up with wet, swollen eyes. "A secret?"

"Yes, it's something the salmon teach us."

"I like salmon. They're yummy." Ripley's eyes grow wide, and her crying ceases.

"I do, too. But they can also show us something valuable, if we watch and observe them. Salmon are amazing and fierce. They also like strong currents. Do you know what that means?"

Ripley shakes her head, wishing her foot would stop throbbing.

"Picture a waterfall, Ripley. Lots of powerful water rushes over a cliff, pulled by gravity. It chugs along at top speed. When water flows like that, it's really a force of nature. Almost nothing or no one can go against that much power."

"Nothing, Mama?"

"Nothing. And really, why should fish like salmon even bother? Why try going against powerful, rushing water?"

"I don't know."

"It would be hard work. *Really hard work*. And if you tried too hard to fight that powerful water, it *could* break you. You could get so tired from going up against something so much stronger than yourself, you could become exhausted, depleted, useless. You might not make it out alive."

"Is that the secret? Salmon love misery?"

"No, my darling." Even at her tender age, Ripley feels relief. She already knew life could be hard. She knew about currents and riptides. And bee stings.

The last glow of orange from the dying sun vanishes. In its place, twinkling stars, as bright as jewels, poke out of a purpling night sky.

"Here's the secret," Sapphire continues. "Most creatures let themselves be directed by what's easy or what others are doing. They let a stream carry them along—not just in the water but in most aspects of life."

"Why?"

Sapphire smiles her warm, protective smile, the one that always cheered up Ripley. "It's easier, *much easier*, to give in to the current, to literally 'go with the flow.' But sometimes, dear Rip, there are things worth striving for."

"I don't want to just do the same easy thing all day."

Sapphire nodded. "I know that about you. It's not in your nature to do what everyone else is doing it. You question things.

"Here's the secret," she continues. "Salmon are truly special fish. They're stronger, smarter, and wiser than they appear. And salmon *don't* let themselves be carried by the current. They swim against it. They use challenges to their advantage. Remember this.

"Salmon, dear chickadee, swim upstream."

(Chickadee is the nickname Sapphire had given Ripley as a young hatchling. As Ripley got older, Sapphire only used it on rare occasions, when no one else was around. Ripley loved how special and safe the gesture made her feel.)

"Salmon plunge past sunken trees. They dive around floating logs, and they even swirl through deadly rapids to lay their eggs," Sapphire continued. "They do the hardest thing, the bravest thing, the thing almost no other fish would do, to give their little ones a better chance to flourish."

Ripley has to think about this for a moment. *Could I be brave like salmon?* Her gaze darts from star to star. Then it hits her. "Hey! My bee sting doesn't hurt anymore."

"You see?" Sapphire winked. "I told you my secret would help."

Ripley sighs, as she nestles her cheek against her mother's warm chest.

"I have one more question, Mama. How do salmon know *when* to fight the current? When to be brave? You aren't telling me to do the opposite of everyone all the time. Right?"

Sapphire chuckles. "No, that's right, chickadee. You should still *try* to listen to those around you, especially when they're trying to help—but within reason." Sapphire winks at her daughter. "Stay curious, use your brain, and do what feels right—to you. Just because things have been one way for a long time doesn't mean they have to stay that way."

Sapphire helps Ripley to her feet. They set off down the grassy hill for home. She stops once more to look her daughter in the eyes. "When things get hard in life, don't be like everyone else. Trust your heart and mind, brave chickadee, as I trust in you. Be the salmon." Sapphire's voice trails off to a whisper.

Ripley can still hear her mom's words from all those years ago as she begins to open her eyes in real time. *Be the salmon. Be the salmon. Be the salmon...*

Before Ripley can see clearly in real life (IRL), she senses someone standing over her. *Mom?* she thinks with hope. She can make out foggy blue tones, a few feathers. But as her eyes focus, the blue tones shift to black. It's clear her mom is nowhere near.

Her vision fully restored, Ripley realizes what's in front of her. It's the last thing on earth she'd ever wanted to see again. That's when she screams.

7

Reximallious Rosenaka...

"No! No. Please, don't eat me." Skidding backward on her bottom, Ripley tries to move away from the terrifying cassowary.

Her eyes are drawn to the beast's dinosaur-like claws and then to the comical red wattles under its chin. The loose skin bounces up and down crazily like a ball on a ping pong paddle. In fact, it springs up and down (and around) so much Ripley worries the cassowary might be trying to hypnotize her. She's almost in a trance again when the strangest thing happens.

The beast speaks. "G'day. How ya doin'?"

Ripley can't believe her ears. She twists her eyebrows in the form of a sideways "S," unable to hide her shock and confusion.

"G'day," he says again in a weirdly friendly, upbeat voice.

Ripley's heart stops pounding in her chest. She squeaks out, "Um, hi?"

"Whatchoo doing? Thinking about salmon, are you?"

Ripley's mind goes blank. *"Salmon?"*

The cassowary walks figure eights around her. As he does, his floppy wattle bobs up and down frantically. "You were saying something about *being the salmon...*"

"Oh, right." Ripley remembers. "That was just something my mom—wait. Hold on! How come you're not eating me right now?"

The cassowary stops walking. "*Should* I be eating you?"

"Yes. I mean no. Please *don't* eat me."

"All right then. I won't."

Ripley is beyond confused. "You mean you *weren't* about to eat me when you just showed up here?"

"That thought had not occurred to me. No."

"Why not?"

"I mean, I *could* eat you. I could commence the formal mastication process, gobbling you up at this very moment. I could probably swallow you whole. Is that the course of action you would most prefer?"

"What? No! Don't eat me."

"Very well. I won't. Unless, of course, you request otherwise. If that's the case, feel free to kindly request I eat you up, and I will try. Posthaste."

This is, without a doubt, the weirdest conversation of Ripley's life. She doesn't know what to make of this oddly polite bird beast. She's pleasantly surprised but still cautious.

"Kidding, kidding. So, back to the salmon." The cassowary resumes his bouncy pacing. "You seemed to be concentrating especially hard on that subject when I first materialized."

"I was dreaming about my mom." Ripley begins to feel at ease talking to the very creature who should frighten her out of her feathers. But the legend can't be totally false. *This bird could change his mind and turn on me at any moment*, she reminds herself. It's best to keep her guard up.

"I have a mom." The perky cassowary flops to the ground with a thump, crossing one long leg over the other.

Now that they are at eye level, Ripley stares at the large, boney crest on the top of the cassowary's head. Vertical and pointy, it reminds her of a shark's fin or a Roman helmet.

"Are you close with your mom?" Ripley asks.

Instead of answering her, the cassowary suddenly drops his head onto the ground. He begins snoring loudly as his big belly rises and falls.

Seconds later, he wakes up with a jolt. "Where was I?"

"I think you just fell asleep...?"

"Indeed, I did. Did you as well?"

"You mean, *did I just fall asleep, too*?"

"Yes, did we just both fall asleep?"

"No."

"You might want to consider it. Just putting it out there."

"But we were just talking. Why would I fall asleep and then wake up one second later?"

The cassowary cocks his head to the side, leans in close, and inspects her with one curious eye—like she's the strange one. "Because it's very refreshing to sleep that way. You should try it."

"Try sleeping for one second?"

"Correct. It's similar to a cat nap. I call it a *cassowary nap*. Though to be perfectly frank with you, the term doesn't roll off the tongue as much as I'd like. Perhaps I will invest some time in coming up with a better name for it—when I'm not cassowary napping, of course."

Ripley says nothing at first. She's baffled by this bizarre creature. "What about cassnap?"

Rex is so focused on his earlier train of thought, he doesn't fully register her remark. "I've seen you before, you know. You work for Banjo."

Ripley's confusion melts away. In its place, she feels pain in her stomach, remembering what just happened with her stash and to her dad—remembering it's all her fault.

"Must be a dreary existence," the cassowary continues. "Diving for anchovies all day long. Then having to hand them over to Banjo with nothing to show for all your hard work."

"I did have something," Ripley says bitterly. "A bounty of anchovies I had been keeping, in case dad ever got really out of sorts and couldn't care for himself. Until Onyx stole them."

"You mean Onyx the seagull?"

"You know him?"

"Oh, I know him all right. And I detest him. He poops on my head far too frequently for my taste. No bowel control on that one, I tell you."

Ripley can't believe her ears. *"He poops? On your head?"*

"Oh, yes. All the time. I will be minding my business, going about my day's activities, when suddenly, his feces will splatter right here on my crest. Sometimes it even gets in my eyes. It's a most disagreeable way to start my morning."

Ripley bursts into a giggle. "Sorry, I shouldn't laugh. That's not polite of me."

"No offense taken, my newfound little blue penguin chum. Speaking of...what's your *nom de plume*?"

"My what?"

"What's your moniker?"

"Hmm?" Ripley still has no idea what he's talking about.

"Please pardon my strange verbal acumen. We cassowaries suffer the affliction of an oversized vocabulary. It's the curse of our species. That and tooting when we sneeze."

"Oh."

"I was asking you for your name."

"Oh, I'm Ripley. What's yours?"

"Reximallious Rosenaka Keperingtellenishmesitercapillarynickomack."

"That's your name?" asks Ripley, incredulous.

"That's the short version anyway."

"That's the *short* version? Seriously?"

"The real version, the one my parents included on my birth certificate, would take several hours to pronounce. Shall we give it a go?"

"Um, can I just call you Rex?"

"Fine. Although I think you are missing out on a wonderful opportunity to expand your linguistic horizons."

Ripley doesn't know what to say to that.

"Anyway, you said Onyx stole your anchovies?"

Ripley nods sadly.

"How many fish are we talking about here?"

"A hundred and fifty."

Rex whistles. “That’s a lot of anchovies. For a little blue penguin to amass, it’s unparalleled. Excuse me.”

Before Ripley can blink, Rex trots away. A second later he returns with a sack of a hundred and fifty anchovies in his beak—her anchovies.

Ripley’s jaw drops to the ground. She can’t believe her eyes. *What in the world?* "How’d you get all my anchovies back? And so fast?”

Rex just shrugs. “We cassowaries can move fast when we want. It’s one of our top skills, besides using big words and taking spectacularly short siestas.”

All the pain in Ripley’s stomach vanishes as she stares at her intact bounty of anchovies. Each fish is still wrapped in a dried banana leaf. “You really got them back!”

Almost as quickly as the pain in Ripley’s stomach had gone away, it returns. With a vengeance. Her stomach lurches. “But Onyx will find out. And when he does, I’m dead meat. Deader than dead meat.”

She frantically pushes them back toward Rex. “You have to give them back!”

Rex stays calm as a cantaloupe. (We assume cucumbers and cantaloupes are equally chill.) “What if I told you there was a way to save all your anchovies? To protect them so no one could take them away?”

8

The Bank Place

"Yikes!" screams Pip, his eyes ready to pop out of their sockets.

"Augggh!" shrieks Shelby.

Just one look at the cassowary is all these two penguin fellas need to convince them that they want nothing to do with this terrifying bird. Before they can retreat to their burrows, Ripley jumps between them and Rex. "Wait! Guys, it's OK. Really." Ripley rests a flipper on Pip's shoulder, her back to Rex.

Pip can't believe his eyes. Neither can Shelby.

On the sandy shore, Ripley remains planted between the boys and the alleged killer beast. Pip's eyes dart about frantically, as his breath becomes quicker and shallower. He's not sure what to think.

"B-b-but that's a cassowary," Pip points out. His whole body starts to tremble.

"A vicious, penguin-eating cassowary," Shelby yells. "Waddle for it!" He turns to flee but stumbles over loose sand and lands on his side. He looks like a toppled-over wind-up toy whose feet keep moving in midair but take him nowhere.

(Sidenote: we've talked before about how little blue penguins don't run. None, that is, except for Ripley. Shelby's plan was for Pip and him to waddle to safety. We'll let you decide if that worked.)

None of that matters now because Rex has opened his enormous beak and swallowed all three penguins. Whole. It turns out cute little penguins really *can't* trust cassowaries, especially not vicious ones named Reximallious Rosenaka Keperingtellenishmesitercapillarynickomack. Rex for short.

Our little blue penguins have died. This is the end of our story.

Just kidding.

Wouldn't this be a terrible book if that really *had* happened? You would be well within your rights as a dissatisfied customer to take this book back to wherever you had purchased it, and demand your money back. But we don't want that. And that's not how our story ends.

No, that's not at all what Rex does. At least not yet.

Surprising both Pip and Shelby, Rex opens his big bird beak...and speaks. "My dear little blue penguin chums, please put away your perfectly justified apprehensions. Though I hail from august cassowary lineage—and members of my species have, from time to time, eaten little blue penguins such as yourselves—I haven't the slightest intention of doing the same."

Pip and Shelby stare up at Rex in disbelief. Pip forgets to blink.

Seeing their shock, Ripley cuts in. "Guys, I was totally freaked out when I first met Rex, too. But I promise you, he's a good guy. He wants to help us."

"Huh?" Shelby grunts.

Pip remains wide-eyed and looks at Ripley.

"You really should blink," Rex says. "Blinking is a wonderful way to keep your eyes moist. The last thing you want at your young age are dry eyes. That condition can lead to all sorts of problems."

None of these words registers with Pip. Paralyzed by fear, he stares at Rex. Somehow his eyes keep widening. The part that used to be white looks like it is covered in thousands of tiny, red lightning bolts.

Finally, his big sister shakes him. "It's OK. Seriously, it is, Pip. Believe me."

The last jolt must have done the trick because Pip finally does blink. Then, he ruffles his shoulder feathers and performs a full body wiggle, eyes now shut. He remembers the shock and disappointment he had felt on this same beach, just a few hours ago. And then he gets mad at Ripley. *Really mad.*

Pip tilts his head and glares at her in disbelief. "How could you and Dad keep all those anchovies for yourselves?"

"Yeah!" Shelby fails to hide any of his own frustration. "You and your dad have been hoarding yummy, delicious anchovies, while the rest of us have been slaving away."

Ripley had worried they might think that. "That's not true. Onyx was lying."

Shelby crosses his flippers across his chest and scowls at Ripley. "Really? You and your dad didn't collect those anchovies to gorge on by yourselves? You want us to believe that? Really?"

"No, we didn't. And stop saying *gorge*."

Pip chimes in. "Gorge. Gorge! My sister loves to stuff her belly. Gorge. Ithaca is gorges. Gorge. What's another name for canyon? Gorge. What word am I saying, Ripley? Gorge. Gorge. Gorge!" Pip's voice grows louder each time he says one of these words. You guessed it—it's GORGE!

(Evidently, all this tough anchovy talk has made Pip forget about the little-blue-penguin-eating cassowary standing right in front of him.)

"Enough!" Ripley yells, as she throws her flippers in the air. "I'll tell you my secret: I was saving those anchovies *for* Dad."

"Why?"

"So he wouldn't have to work so hard. He hasn't been meeting his quota as it is. And I didn't want him to feel like he was failing at one more thing. He's been so sad—sadder than you think—since we lost Mom. I didn't think Dad could do it alone, and now with an open wound on his shoulder, he really can't."

Shelby and Pip lock eyes. They're once again fearful.

"B-but saving is not allowed," says Pip.

"Yeah. Banjo forbids it," Shelby adds.

Exhausted, Ripley flops down on the beach. She's ten, and yet she feels tired. *Really tired.* Like old lady penguin tired. "It was a stupid idea. I admit it."

Rex flops down beside her. His big bird rump kicks up clouds of sand, and the light brown haze that follows blinds the group. When it settles, to Pip and Shelby's surprise, they notice Rex has put his enormous black wing around Ripley's shoulders. "The only thing stupid about what you did is to call it *stupid*."

"Huh?"

Rex jumps up. As all three little blue penguins watch slack-jawed, Rex runs up and down the beach. "Don't you see?" he says, still running. "Yours is an untenable situation. A travesty of outrageous proportions."

"What is?" Ripley asks.

"Your very *lives*, mates. You and your loved ones are toiling away. All day, every day: swimming, diving, collecting—then giving it all away to that perfectly villainous scamp: Banjo."

"We also do a bit of eating and barfing daily," Pip generously points out.

"I prefer the eating after the barfing," says Shelby, winking at Ripley to remind her of their earlier debate. She smiles back at him but rolls her eyes, too.

"Forget about all that. You don't have to live that way. You can be..." Rex spreads his completely useless wings and says, "*free*."

Rex waits for Shelby and Pip to applaud his brilliant idea. Instead, they burst out laughing. Now Ripley is the one who's upset.

"What are you two laughing at? Rex's right."

Ripley doesn't bother to tell them she has no idea how they can possibly pull this off. But she likes the way Rex is talking. There must be a better way. She smiles for him to go on.

"Let me paint a picture for you," he says. "There is a place. A wondrous place replete with vaults and locks and loads and loads of security. It's called a bank and, listen here, my fellow flightless friends. This place—*this bank*—holds the very key to your emancipation."

"Our *what*?" Shelby asks.

Pip sneezes and toots at the same time. "Excuse me."

"Your freedom, mates. Have you ever seen the back of the huge sign on the beach that reads 'Catching Your Quota = Freedom'? It has some very interesting verbiage. I'm paraphrasing here, but you are only beholden to Banjo until you amass five thousand anchovies."

"Excuse me? Could you repeat that in Penguinish, please? *Only* five thousand anchovies for what?" Pip requests.

"My apologies again. Yes, gather five thousand anchovies for Banjo, and you'll never owe him another fish. Ever."

"I like the sound of that!" Shelby interjects. "Never having to share my grub again would be...scrumptious!" He licks the sharp edge of his beak.

Ripley is more hesitant. "You make that sound so simple, Rex. Five thousand anchovies all at once, especially when we aren't allowed to save, would be impossible! It took me months to save just a hundred and fifty. It was so risky. And I practically lost them to Onyx, plus that's..." She pauses, running a calculation in her head. "Woah. Five thousand is over thirty-three times the size of my savings! No way we could save that many!"

"Sharp math skills, Little Blue." Rex pauses. "I like the sound of that moniker. Mind if I call you that? But additionally, I'd like to point out that you didn't *actually* lose your savings. I did recover the stash for you, right?"

Ripley nods.

"Those thinking skills will continue to serve you well, now and down the road. Take heed, math is a very important skill set. But, yes, you have a point. Gathering five thousand anchovies, all on your own, would be immensely difficult, potentially impossible, and extremely treacherous. First things first. Let me take a step back.

"You see, long ago, in the annals of animal lore, a since-deceased creature came to this conclusion: Anchovies have value, and they can be traded. You can buy and sell them. Lots of animals want them.

"They also hold most of their value over time." (We are assuming there are relatively low rates of inflation when this story takes place.) "Sure, you can catch an anchovy or two and eat it that day. They can be delicious, especially when they're at their freshest. But uneaten anchovies are still worth something tomorrow." (Sidenote: If you guessed anchovies were the animal version of money or gold, 6,243 bonus points for you!)

Rex goes on. "Some wise little penguins might decide to save a few extra fishies for a rainy day." Rex winks at Ripley, and she swells with joy.

"And, as we know so well, because anchovies are valuable, others may want them, and still others will try to steal them. You can't just bury them underground and assume they'll be there in the morning, right? I mean, Onyx just stole your loot, Little Blue."

Ripley nods.

"There is, however, one place where you can store anchovies—somewhere safe, that is. A bank."

Shelby's tummy grumbles. "All this anchovy talk has made me hungry."

Ripley has a thought. "Does Banjo know about this...bank place?"

"Of course he does, Little Blue. I don't know a single wealthy animal or business owner who doesn't frequent a bank. I'm almost certain Banjo deposits a bunch of the anchovies you give him directly in a bank. Plus, there's no way he could possibly partake of such voluminous largesse on his own. Not without severe gastric externalities and the imminent threat of losing all his wealth."

"What is he saying?" Pip asks Shelby and Ripley, totally lost.

"He means Banjo already knows about the bank place. That's where he keeps his own stash and probably lots of the anchovies we catch for him every day. He saves things," Ripley translates.

Rex smiles upon her with pride. "Bingo."

"You mean *Banjo*?" Pip asks.

"No. Bingo. It's a common idiom—oh, forget it. Your clever sister is absolutely right. Banjo has long known of this place, the bank, and more to the point, he's kept its very existence a secret from you little blue penguins."

Something doesn't feel right to Ripley. "Wait a minute. Even if this is true, why are *you* helping *us*? Is there something in this for you? Are you trying to steal back our anchovies?"

Suddenly, Shelby and Pip want to know the very same thing.

For once, Rex looks tongue-tied. "I have my reasons. But no. Without a doubt, I have no interest in your anchovies. Those are yours, fair and square."

Ripley's mind works at warp speed. "I saw you this morning. You were on the beach when I tried to find my dad before lineup. Weren't you? Were you spying on us?"

Rex looks offended. "*Spying* is a vulgar word. *Surveilling* is much more civilized."

"You *were* spying on us! But what I don't get is why. And speaking of *why*, why don't you eat us all up? That's what the legends say cassowaries do."

"Are you crazy?" Pip yells. "Don't tell him to eat us!"

Just to be on the safe side, he and Shelby start backing away.

Now, Rex looks really offended. "How dare you think I would deign to eat you. I will have you know that I...am a vegetarian."

"A veggie what?"

"I don't eat meat. Never have. Honestly, I find the very thought repulsive."

"Then what do you eat?" Ripley asks.

"Bottlebrush. Bit of blueberry lily when I can find it. I also enjoy eucalyptus. From time to time, I will indulge in Geraldton waxflowers. I can even go for a bit of swamp lily, if I'm in the mood."

"You promise you won't eat us?" Pip asks.

"Promise."

"Pinky promise?"

"Do you have a pinky?" Rex asks.

"No. But I can still pinky promise. If *you* will."

All three little blue penguins wait for Rex's answer.

"I will not eat you up," he says. "Pinky promise." Rex points his enormously sharp, prehistoric toe toward Pip's chest.

Pip looks like he'll faint, but he doesn't. Instead, he slowly lifts his flipper to touch Rex's deadly dagger. "Pin-ky pro-mise." Pip sounds out each syllable before finally breathing a sigh of relief.

As soon as that's out of the way, Ripley turns to Rex. "Now, about my anchovy stash: Can you take us to this bank?"

9

Bank Run

We're doing this! Ripley thinks. *I can't believe we're really doing this.* Her next thought is: *We better get to the bank and back to the burrow before sunrise. We have work tomorrow.*

Thankfully, our little blue penguins have the right transportation, if you can call him that. Ripley, Shelby, and Pip are perched on top of Rex's back. And, boy, does this cassowary move. At top speed, Rex clocks in at 30 miles per hour.

He's fast. Like lightning fast. We're talking bullet-train velocity.

Dear reader, have you ever seen a cheetah in the wild who's chasing a gazelle? No? That makes sense. You probably haven't grown up in the safari. Hmm. OK. Have you ever watched the Earth zoom around the sun? No? That makes sense, too. You probably haven't experienced outer space. All right.

We haven't either. But that sounds pretty darn fast.

We're not sure if Rex is *that* fast.

But he is one speedy cassowary. And he certainly outpaces waddling little blue penguins any day of the week.

What's more amazing? While bolting from southern Australia's lovely beaches over its grassy hills at a breathtaking clip, Rex manages to carry on deep conversation.

"Precisely how much thought have you given to the subject of time?" he asks the three feathered friends riding on his back.

"Time?" Ripley grips Rex's black feathers, hanging on for dear life.

Beside her, Shelby's already puffy cheeks balloon like bullfrogs as he bounces on Rex's back. He can taste some of yesterday's sour, half-digested dinner but manages to keep it down.

"Time," Rex continues. "In my humble opinion, it's the world's most valuable resource."

"What's a resource?" Pip is so tiny that he ricochets up and down between Rex's shoulders like popcorn in the microwave.

"Ooh, glad you should ask! Let me try to put this in terms you might understand. A resource is something that has value. It's something we can use. You might recall our prior conversation. But time is different from other resources. It doesn't have value *exactly* in the way that gold or anchovies do. Time is so special because we can't get more of it. So we must choose wisely how we spend this time."

"Huh?" Shelby shoots Pip a quizzical look. "So I can't go anywhere to buy time. But if someone wants to pay me in anchovies, I'd happily give them some of mine!"

"Spot on, Shelby. It generally can't be bought or sold the way anchovies or gold can. It's not a physical thing."

"But we can trade our time for money or anchovies. For example, you could work for a boss and get paid for your time. Your case with Banjo is particularly cruel because he doesn't compensate you well (well, not at all!) for your work."

All three little blue penguins listen intently.

As Rex's voice trails off, he veers slightly to the right, like someone who's been texting and driving.

Then, abruptly, Rex stops to let a turtle driving a green truck cross the road. The truck is etched with a modern logo and font that spells DAINTREE. Large brown paper packages peek out of its roof.

"That turtle was in some hurry," Rex exclaims before peering over his shoulder, his eye just inches from Ripley's, Shelby's, and Pip's little faces. His shiny eyeball is almost as big as Ripley's head, and she can see Pip's baffled expression mirrored in it.

"I digress from my general explanation. Pardon me. Bad habit. There's just so much to think about, so much to share." Rex takes a long, slow, deep breath that fills his lungs, causing his chest to swell. He smiles again with excitement, a sparkle in his eye.

"Let's go a bit further. Have you ever heard of the time value of money? Or how about compound interest?"

The three shake their heads 'no.'

"No worries. That's to be expected. The earlier you understand some of these magical concepts, however, the better. Shelby, what would you say if I gave you ten anchovies right now?

"Are you serious?" Shelby's eyes light up.

"Dead serious, mate."

"That would be amazing! You'd be my new best friend—well, after Ripley, of course. I'd scarf them all down—"

"But what if, instead, I gave you eleven anchovies next month? And if you left the anchovies with me, I'd keep giving you more anchovies over time? Even anchovies for the last anchovies you had received from me?"

"I'd still take the ten now, thank you very much," says Shelby. Rex isn't surprised.

"I'd wait," Ripley chimes in.

"Of course you would," Shelby teases. "But seriously, what good would it do me to save for the future, even if you promised me more, when I'm hungry right now? Like this very instant? I'm literally starving all the time."

"Understandable, Shelby. Very understandable. It's definitely harder to save when we don't earn that much, and we work just to survive," Rex concedes.

"Plus, what would I even want to save for?" Shelby asks. "My family doesn't need my help. We each fish our quota."

"I certainly hope they never do," Ripley quips.

"Didn't mean to insult, Ripley. Sorry."

Ripley smiles understandingly.

"There are struggles we might face in the future. To be prepared for these, savings can prove immensely liberating," Rex says. "Additionally, perhaps there are things you'd like to do or buy down the road—things you haven't even thought of yet! An um...uh..." Rex pauses to think. "Oh! A fancier meal perhaps. Or how about a slightly larger burrow? Or maybe you'd like a life more like Banjo's. Your life could look very different from how it does now if you saved...and invested."

"Not as long as we're slaves to Banjo," Ripley counters.

"I couldn't agree more, Little Blue." Rex smiles a sharp-beaked grin toward Ripley and winks. "I think you should keep saving some of your catch for a later date."

Pip has stayed quiet until now. Pip pipes up. "Noooo, guys! This is all totally risky. Remember Onyx? I can't imagine what Banjo might do if he catches us!"

Rex continues undeterred. "I hear you, my fine boy. But let's face the facts and consider what I see as a life-altering opportunity. Banjo is an uber-villain who threatens your very well-being. He wants to keep you chained to him forever, and he's fed you utter lies to do it. Lie number one: Cassowaries are the enemy. But I'm not. Agreed?"

All three bob their heads in acceptance.

"Don't you see, Pip and Shelby? Ripley is truly on to something. Something BIG," Rex declares. "Saving little bits over time can add up to a huge amount. Just look at Ripley's bounty, saved over the course of months."

Pip shakes his head and mouths to Ripley again, "I'm scared, Ripley. Is he trying to get us killed? Banjo and his henchman are scary."

With his flipper he secretively motions crazy circles around his ear, so Rex can't see. Pip still wonders if he truly can trust Rex.

"This is it, Ripley. We can save your stash of anchovies but not again. Pleeease. I don't want to lose you like we did Mom. I need you. Dad needs you."

"I won't let you down, Pip. Promise. Let's just hear him out," Ripley responds quietly.

"Now here's the real kicker. Listen closely," Rex continues. "Banjo's lie number two: You are chained to him forever. You do have a way out, in fact. We just need to get you a whole lot of anchovies at once. Thanks to the time value of money you can invest, and your savings can grow exponentially—with enough time and interest. Oh, my goodness! Oh, my goodness! This is so exciting, friends! Don't you think?"

(Sidenote: Get ready for finance to Blow. Your. Mind. This stuff could literally change your life. Crazy animal action to resume shortly.)

"Time is central to this utter investing magic. You can supercharge your savings by leveraging time and compound interest! AHHHHHH! Can you think of anything cooler? Or more powerful? This is just beyond!"

Shelby hears his stomach rumble with hunger. Pip feels queasy and overwhelmed, and he starts to sway like a falling leaf. This is too much for him to think about.

But Ripley has barely blinked since Rex started talking. This is the most intellectually stimulated she has been in years. She can't wait to learn more.

Rex is so worked up that he runs even faster. With each leap, he bounds farther. He's entered a flow state. His speech continues to accelerate like a plane before lift-off. Ripley catches most of what he's saying, but Rex peppers them with new terms and concepts so quickly. *Interest rates...index funds...stocks...returns...P/E ratios...risk/reward...savings and brokerage accounts...*

Pip and Shelby don't follow. Their eyes glaze over.

Rex realizes he has given his friends a bit too much at once.

***

"This would all be easier to show you, but until we have that chance, I'll try to summarize," Rex suggests.

"In a nutshell, when I save," Rex says, "I delay using something today to have some more in the future. I can give my money to a bank or invest it somewhere—in a company, for example. The bank promises to give it back—plus a little extra—in the future. We call that 'little extra' interest.

"When I invest in a company or several companies, there is some risk of loss but also a greater potential reward than with a savings account. We call the reward or money I can receive from investments a return."

"That sounds mega-dangerous," squeaks Pip. He's confused. "Why would I work my flippers off to save, then invest, and maybe even lose it all?!"

"Ehh," mutters Shelby. "I'd rather splash with my friends than worry about this investing schminvesting stuff."

But Ripley's still completely entranced. She feels like Rex is the first being since her mom who might truly get her. "What kind of risk?" she asks, still cautious. "Like someone could break my arm or run me over?"

"No, no, Little Blue," Rex chuckles. "I wouldn't recommend uncivilized investments like that! No deals with gangsters! At least no new ones. Speaking of gangsters, we need to get you untangled from Banjo. Stat.

"What I mean by risk/reward is that you will mostly likely gain but could also *lose* some anchovies. I have to be completely honest. Certain investments, like stocks, index funds, and mutual funds, will go up and down. Often the greater the risk, the greater the possible return. But with the right investments, things work out well over time."

"I don't like risk. I want to be cozy and comfortable, even if we're not rich. I like our simple lives. No need to change. Too much effort. Too hard!" Pip exclaims.

"I hear you, Pip. Trying something new can be scary. And I understand that even the thought of risk can push some penguins, like you, Pip, away from investing altogether. That's an absolute shame.

"Think about this. Aren't you taking a risk when you wake up? How about when you fish? You could be eaten by a shark at sea—or pulled away by a rip current. But you still swim and fish every day.

"Investing involves a different version of risk. Why not give it a small chance and see if you can navigate it, kind of the way you do the sea turtles, the dolphins, and even Banjo?" Rex pleads.

Despite her desire to learn more, Ripley feels a sudden jolt of skepticism. She thinks of her present situation and life circumstance. "But...Banjo would have our heads!" Ripley panics.

"For now, it would appear he might try to take them regardless, Little Blue," Rex responds. "Not enough people—or penguins—know the rules of this investing game. Or they think this game—which I do thoroughly love and think you will, too—isn't made for them. I believe you just need someone to help guide you, someone with whom you can navigate new investing territory. Then you need to test the waters yourselves. And finally, I hope you might even enjoy it."

"But Banjo would kill us!" Pip repeats as he melts down in tears. Rex's attempted pep talk isn't going over well with everyone.

In a calmer, more serious voice, Rex persists. "The biggest missed opportunity I see in finance—sorry, in investing—possibly even life, is choosing to avoid it completely. I can help get you out of your mess.

"**Step one**: Save what you can.

"**Step two**: Place that savings (money or anchovies) into a bank.

"**Step three**: Choose wise investments that will allow your savings to grow and multiply over time."

"Grow?" Ripley likes the sound of that.

"They'll truly get bigger? The anchovies? But they're dead!" Shelby chimes in.

"Ha ha, not quite. Anchovies and money can grow in value, but they won't physically get bigger, no. Sincerest apologies, Shelby. I like to think of it this way: Farmers need time to grow plants. We can't just plant a seed in the ground and poof—get a beautiful flower."

"Oh, right!" offers Pip, pleasantly distracted from his earlier fears. "But what does a flower need to grow?"

"It needs water, soil, air, sunlight, nutrients, and time. Think of your investments and savings as seeds that need protection, access to sound inputs (water and nutrients), and time." says Rex.

Ripley has another question. "OK, I love the sound of this, but why would a bank protect our anchovies and give us more? Wouldn't we owe them something for protecting our savings?"

"I like the inquisitive skepticism, Rip. Bring it on, Little Blue!" cheers Rex. "Banks need anchovies just like you need anchovies. Only instead of eating them, banks invest as well. They might lend money to other animals for things like starting a business or buying a home, for example. In return, the borrowers of that money end up owing the bank interest. Banks will also charge an occasional fee for maintenance or certain transactions, like special deliveries of your money.

"The longer you keep your anchovies at a bank, let's say in a savings account, the more you help them. It's a form of cooperation. The bank gives you a few additional anchovies for your savings account to say thank you and to keep you 'interest-ed'." Rex motions scare-quotes with his dagger toes, mid-stride. "See what I did there?" Rex winks. He likes winking, Ripley has noticed.

Shelby licks his lips. "If I were a bank, I would eat those anchovies. Every last one."

Pip squeaks. "Remind me never to bank with you."

Ripley ignores them both. Her brain is on fire. "So let's say we put these hundred and fifty anchovies into—what did you call it? A savings account? And then we wait a bit, and we'd have thousands of them?"

"Not likely! Another good question on interest rates and returns, Ripley." Rex is about to explain more when they burst through a web. He feels a spider tickling his beak and has to flick it off. "Banks don't usually pay that much interest just to keep your anchovies safe—"

"See. Told you. We should just eat them," says Shelby.

"For that," Rex continues, "you would have to invest in other things, let's say public companies through things called stocks or shares. You can literally own a small piece of a company, if you want."

Somehow, the spiders continued to hang on to Rex's beak. Ripley doesn't want to be rude, so she and the others don't say anything about Rex's eight-legged guest. But it's a definite distraction.

"Before I tell you more about investments, I have one last reminder about time," says Rex. "Since you're young, time can work serious magic for you. You will likely live much longer than I. The more time you have to invest your anchovies, the greater your investments can grow—exponentially, in fact. This is thanks to time and the concept of compound interest, concepts that are truly powerful. And *that* will set you free."

"Free?" Ripley sits up taller on Rex's back.

"Yes, you could free yourself of any debt to Banjo. At some point, you wouldn't owe him another anchovy. You'd have freedom from having to dive all day for him. Freedom from mean Tasmanian devils. Freedom to do what you want, when you want. Financial freedom spells, well, in your case, actual *freedom!*"

With his head high in the air, Rex takes one enormous breath before, shockingly, he keels over. The little penguins slide straight off his shoulders and onto the dusty ground with a tremendous thud.

Once Ripley recovers, she checks on Pip and Shelby. "Are you guys OK?"

"Yeah. But what was that, Rip?" asks Shelby, rubbing the side of his head. "Where's Rex? Why did we stop so suddenly?"

Still dizzy from the fall, Ripley turns and eyes Rex a few feet away. He's splayed out on his side like an oversized dog basking in a sun puddle. She waddles closer before noticing that he's motionless. Ripley can't see Rex's breathing. He doesn't even blink.

10

Trapped

"No—" Ripley gasps, covering her mouth with her flipper. "I can't lose you, too."

Shelby waddles in frantic little circles, repeating the same phrase: "Rex is dead. Rex is dead."

Ripley hugs her friend. She wipes her eyes so no one can see her tears.

"Wait. Where's Pip?"

Petrified, Ripley looks for him among the tall grasses. "Pip. Where are you?"

"I thought you told me he was OK, Shel!" begs Ripley.

"Oh, I was only answering for myself." Shelby quickly retorts before pacing and muttering to himself again.

Amid all the "Rex is dead" talk, Ripley detects something low and muffled.

"Pip? Pip! Is that you?"

There it is again. "Mmhkhmhm" is all Ripley can make out. Or maybe it's "Mmmkh." Or "Mmmghmm." We're no experts in muffled speaking.

"Pip?"

"I'm here. Under Rex," she finally gleans from all that mumbling.

Then it hits her: Rex must have collapsed on top of little Pip when he toppled over.

She grabs Shelby's shoulder. "We have to pry Rex off Pip. Rex's crushing him."

Shelby shakes his head. "I can't do that."

"Why not?"

"I've never touched anything dead before."

"So what?"

"What if I catch what Rex got? What if I die, too?"

Ripley rolls her eyes. "If you don't hurry, Pip *will* die. Now help me, please."

Before Shelby can say no again, Ripley pulls him by the flipper. Together, they push and push the cassowary with all their might.

And...nothing happens. Pip remains trapped beneath Rex.

"It stinks under here, you guys." Pip's voice is momentarily clearer.

"Bad?" Shelby asks.

"Really bad," says Pip.

"How bad?"

"Really, really bad."

"How bad is bad?"

"Um. It's kind of like wet dog mixed with dirty belly button."

"That *is* bad."

"Who cares how bad it smells!" Ripley implores. "We're wasting time."

Again, she and Shelby try to lift Rex. They can only manage to boost him a centimeter off the ground. Cassowaries are big birds and Shelby and Ripley, well, they're tiny blue ones, as you know. Exhausted, the two *pingüinos* collapse into a heap on the ground.

"This is hopeless," says Shelby. "Also, Rex is dead. Dead! How did this all happen?"

Ripley isn't the kind of kid to admit defeat. Not ever. She's done hard things and faced insane challenges in her life. Lots of them. You know that. We know that. Crazy hard.

But even she feels momentarily beaten. The three vulnerable penguins are miles away from their burrow with absolutely no clue about their surroundings, let alone how to seek shelter. They're toast without Rex's protection and transportation. To boot, Pip is trapped under the very creature—the very dead as a doornail, dead as a doorknob, dead as a whatever-you-want-to-call-it, plain dead creature—who brought them here in the first place.

Wherever *here* is.

"What'll we do now?" Shelby asks.

Ripley notices he's eating one of the anchovies from her stash. "Hey!"

"Leave me alone. I need to eat when I'm nervous." He can barely breathe between bites.

"Those anchovies belong in an account! I worked so hard for them," Ripley says.

Shelby snorts as he lifts his head from his fishy flippers. "Um, not to be rude, but now that Rex is dead, the odds of our ever finding that bank he told us about are slim to none. Plus, aren't some of these going to go bad in the heat?"

Ripley wants to argue, but he's right—about all of it. She sighs sadly.

"So are you guys getting me out of here like *soon*? Or can you wrap up your party and lift me loose? Please? Pretty please? With a cherry on top—whatever that means?"

Ripley doesn't have the heart to tell Pip that the answer is a big fat 'no.' She and Shelby won't be able to get him out. They just can't physically do it.

"All right then?" Shelby tries to stand.

Then they look up to see a bizarre sight walking toward them. It must be a mirage, something they've imagined. *How hard did they hit their heads anyway*? they think.

Ripley believes she sees a gray-and-white wallaby in a suit and tie. He carries a briefcase with his long tail.

"Nice afternoon isn't it, children?"

"I think I've gone mad, Shel," Ripley whispers to Shelby. "Is that a talking wallaby? With a suitcase?"

The wallaby pays no mind. He notices Rex and continues. "A dead cassowary. Don't see that every day, do you? All right then. I best be off. Time is money, you know. I should be at work."

"Wait." Ripley throws herself in front of him. "You ARE real! Could you help us save our friend? Pleeease."

The wallaby looks at her sadly. "Of course, I'm real," he scoffs. "But afraid I can be of no assistance, missy. Nothing doing. That fella's dead as a doorknob. If only I'd gotten here sooner. Sincerest apologies." The wallaby lowers his head a moment, to respect the deceased. "Right then, off I go. Good day, chums," he continues, as if this were any normal day with only normal events.

Shelby stops him. "No, please, sir. You don't understand. My friend's *under* the cassowary."

The wallaby's dark eyes narrow suspiciously. "Is this a trap? What the devil is your mate doing under a dead cassowary?"

"Rex, the cassowary, our friend, fell on my little brother Pip when he died. Pip's been trapped there ever since."

The wallaby is unmoved. "Are you two having a laugh? Who's ever heard of a friendship between a penguin and a cassowary? Don't believe it for one second. I'll have you know I am not in the mood for childish games from silly kids, who, I might add, should be in school. Now I truly must attend to pressing business matters. Off I go."

Ripley won't let up. She blocks his path. "We're not playing games. My little brother is underneath poor Rex. Aren't you, Pip?"

"Yes. And it smells like gym socks mixed with wombat snot in here."

The wallaby's features light up. "Great white whale! Strangest thing. My word! You *weren't* pulling my tail. Why didn't you just come out and say so?"

"We *did* say so."

The wallaby is distracted again. "I told you I'm a busy wallaby." He straightens his little tie and starts to go. "If you don't mind, I'll be on my way."

Ripley catches him by his fuzzy wallaby shoulder. "Please, sir."

"Oh, all right. But call me Ignatius, dear. All my banker friends do."

A *bank*, Ripley thinks. But she can't focus on that now. She has bigger problems. "Sir—I mean Ignatius—we're all alone out here. My brother's trapped."

"Yes, I know. We covered that part earlier. Curious tale. One for the ages. But I really must be on my way—"

"Can you help us move him? Please?"

Ignatius stops. "Why didn't you just ask me that in the first place? You little blue penguins do beat around the bush, don't you? Very well then."

The wallaby carefully places his briefcase on the ground. Ignatius pulls a small but powerful tool from his otherwise tiny satchel.

"This is how you do it. Just use this handy jack. One never knows when one will need to change a tire or, in this case, lift a cassowary. Best to be prepared for a rainy day, I always say!"

Crank, crank, crank, squeeeeaaak! The jack lifts Rex a few feet off the ground.

Squished, flattened, and frightened, but finally freed, Pip can't believe his eyes. He wriggles out from under Rex's heavy body and throws his arms around his big sister. "I thought I'd never escape."

Ignatius leaves Rex propped against a tree with the greatest of care before taking his briefcase in paw. "Now, unless there are more penguin pickles to untangle, I must resume my afternoon's duties. I bid you *adieu*."

Ripley still doesn't want to let the wallaby go. Ever since she spied his briefcase and heard him speak of money, time, and banker friends, she's been curious about him.

"Ignatius, are you on your way to a bank now?"

"Quite so, my dear. How'd you know?"

"Just a guess. Thanks again a million for your help," Ripley says.

"Glad to do it, my dear. It was a worthy cause."

"W-w-would you mind if we followed you? We're a bit lost," Ripley asks cautiously.

"As you wish. Just try to keep up, please. I'm now in a dreadful hurry."

Ripley motions to Shelby and Pip for assistance as she hoists the bag of anchovies over one shoulder. Then they all follow Ignatius. After about half a mile, they arrive at an intersection—Broadway and Wallaby Street. Ignatius pivots sharply on one foot, takes a right turn, and heads down Wallaby Street. The three little blue penguins follow closely behind.

II

The Piggy Bank

"Stop right there."

Ripley tilts her head way back to see whose deep voice could be booming at her from overhead. Moments ago, she, Shelby, and Pip had arrived with Ignatius, the all-business-all-the-time Wallaby, at the Piggy Bank. Rather fittingly, the building is situated at 10 South Wallaby Street.

Standing before a pair of grand doors that mark the entrance to the bank, the blue feather friends stare at kangaroos the size of basketball players. (Sidenote: Ripley probably doesn't know who basketball players are. She doesn't even know what basketball is. Our analogy would confuse her. Luckily, you're the ones reading this book. But here's a translation for blue penguins anyway: These dudes are super tall.)

Ripley looks way, way up to find one kangaroo's face. And honestly? What she sees isn't a soft face. It's a hardened, stern face. It's kind of angular and expressionless. *Okay, fine.* It's the kind of face that makes people stop and say, "Yikes. That's one intimidating dude."

It's a good bet this tall, scary guy has heard others say unkind things like that his whole life. That's our assumption because this kangaroo doesn't exude warmth either. Or kindness. He means serious business. How serious? Like I-will-punch-you-in-the-face-and-take-your-bike-*and*-your-Halloween-candy-if-you-cross-me serious.

Plus, he's wearing boxing gloves.

All the kangaroos—Ripley counts seven in total—wear boxing gloves. Red and huge, the more Ripley looks at their oversized leather hand pillows, the more she's certain these beasts could knock her out in an instant.

Why are they here, you ask? These towering kangaroos are the Piggy Bank's muscle. They're the bank's first line of security, put in place to protect important things that animals deposit there—like money and anchovies. (Another word for these important things is assets. Ahem, no, that's not a swear word, in case you were wondering. Assets are things of value, like money and gold and other investments.)

Again, these kangas are meant to frighten off potential robbers, thieves, hackers, etc. before they can even think about making a sneaky move. Modern-day bank security for humans does not look exactly like this, as you might imagine. Instead, you would likely find a badged security guard at the entrance of an actual bank. There could even be a retina scan or facial recognition software involved in protecting the bank and its customers, too.

If you bank online, you could be required to provide several layers of information—usernames, passwords, personal information, and even one-time generated codes, each and every time you want to log on. All that to say, bank security is a big deal and even a business of its own. (That's a good thing. Agreed?)

Now back to the main kangaroo in front of Ripley. This guard barks a command at Ripley as she gets closer. "Not so fast. Where'd you think you's is going?"

(Kangaroo security guards often struggle with grammar. Maybe their teachers didn't cover subject-verb agreement at kangaroo college or wherever it is these guys went to school. Come to think of it, Kangaroo Academies probably focuses exclusively on how to punch someone in the face if a robber were to make a suspicious move at a bank.)

"'Ullo there, Franklin. These chums are with me," Ignatius puts in. Our wallaby is apparently on a first-name basis with this big thug.

At that, Franklin moves aside, permitting the three little blue penguins to pass. Still, he snarls at them for good measure. That's to be expected, though. He is just doing his job.

The moment Ripley steps into the bank lobby, she's stunned. Is she truly here? Are any of them, or is this just another dream? She can't help but think of poor Rex. She had only known Rex briefly, like just for a few hours, but they were on the brink of something special together. She just knew it.

Besides, she hadn't be able to thank him. Had she forced him to his death? He had died trying to help her. It pains her to have left him where he had perished suddenly, leaning against that lonely tree.

He should be here with us, Ripley thinks.

Still entranced, she continues viewing the lobby with awe. It's magical and overwhelming with its floor-to-ceiling marble columns and its pristine, white walls. This place is what Rex had wanted to show her.

It's bustling like a train station on a Tuesday morning. Naturally, she hasn't much time to sulk. A parade of animals zooms past in a flash. The pack includes a sugar glider (holding a teetering stack of paper receipts). There's also something called an echidna. This guy looks like a cross between a porcupine and an anteater and wears a blue cotton jacket. He talks feverishly and loudly on his cell phone.

"Buy, buy, buy, I tell you. This thing has nowhere to go but up. Best fundamentals of any company this century. Zero potential downside, as far as I can tell. I want fifty thousand shares ASAP," the echidna exclaims as he spins around and zips off in another direction.

Mr. Echidna exudes even more self-confidence than Franklin out front. Yet he doesn't scare Ripley. Still, it's not like she would want to share tea with him either.

Ignatius, ever in a hurry, passes them and forges on.

Trying her best to keep pace, Ripley spies a platypus, that bizarre creature we covered back in Chapter 1. Has it been that long? My, how time flies when you're going on a journey with little blue penguins, eager to deposit anchovies in a bank—an institution that's run by pigs and guarded by kangaroos!

This particular platypus sports a smart pair of tortoise-shell glasses. He must also know Ignatius because the two grown-ups exchange nods. Like most of the other animals flanking him, this flat-billed creature waits patiently in line.

But not Ignatius.

Ignatius isn't a wallaby to put up with lines. He's a VIP. (Or maybe we should say VIW, a.k.a. "very important wallaby.") After greeting his friend, he just keeps on trucking. Shelby struggles to keep up. Then Ripley and Pip fall behind and almost get trampled by a giant emu.

This tall bird does not appreciate anyone, let alone little blue penguins, who cut in front of her in line.

"Hey," the emu hisses, her head tilted to one side so that she can gape at them with one of her enormous, shiny eyes. While Rex would sometimes also lower his head in conversation, this gal is S-C-A-R-Y.

A bit of emu spittle hits Shelby smack in the face. The penguins duck beneath her, squeezing between her long legs to keep up with Ignatius. By now, Ignatius is practically racing to the teller's kiosk.

Tellers, in case you didn't know, are those people—or in this case, those animals—who handle certain bank transactions like deposits and withdrawals. (If you deposit money [or anchovies], you add them to an account. In the case of withdrawals, you take money [or anchovies] out.)

Incidentally, tellers are often the ones who get robbed when bad guys burst into banks in movies, demanding money—hence the need for kangaroo guards with boxing gloves. Obviously.

Shelby continues to wipe sticky goop from his forehead. Watching this makes Ripley shudder, and she realizes that he must smell terrible, too—maybe like a spider monkey's armpit. (Take our word for it. It's repulsive.)

At last, the trio reunites with Ignatius, just as he reaches an open bank kiosk. The wallaby stops strutting and comes to an abrupt halt. Unfortunately, Shelby hadn't noticed the desk, and smacks right into it. "Ouch!" he grunts, rubbing the bridge of his beak.

A few feet overhead, on the other side of a semi-circle counter made of polished marble, sits a very stout pig. He has a bubble-gum pink complexion (to be expected), a saucer-like nose (also expected, right?), and in that nose, two gaping holes. These are his nostrils. On his round body he wears a sharp-looking, custom-tailored shirt and suit.

"I can't see," Ripley whispers to Shelby. Without wasting a second, Shelby stacks Pip and then Ripley onto his shoulders.

"That's better. Thanks, Shel." Now Ripley can catch a glimpse over the counter at our porky teller, uh...sorry, we mean piggy banker.

Ignatius hands the teller some papers. After the pink pig takes them, he types rapidly on a computer as if he were a concert pianist performing a piece by Beethoven. Then he hands Ignatius a slip in return and asks, "Anything else for you today, sir?"

The teller's not as tall as the kangaroos, but he's equally serious. That must be a job requirement of the Piggy Bank, come to think of it. His facial expression remains frozen. Deep furrows from a lifetime of frowning connect his beady little pig eyes.

"Appreciate it, Connor. There is something else," says Ignatius, addressing the pig. "These young'uns want a word with you. Could you stitch them up, ol' chap?"

Connor glares at the three little blue friends, moving only his eyes as he does so.

"Connor? Be a good mate now, and help them with their question. As a favor to me. Please," says Ignatius.

"You 'ave business with our bank?" Connor grunts at Shelby, as the pig peers down at him over the counter. The teller must think Shelby's in charge, since he's the biggest of the three penguins and a boy. But he's wrong.

"Um." That's all Shelby can think to say.

Ripley leans forward with a hundred and fifty anchovies wrapped in bananas leaves. Strike that. A hundred and forty-eight anchovies. Remember Shelby ate some earlier to help calm his nerves.

"Hello, sir. I wish to open a..." Ripley starts.

Oh, no. Ripley has forgotten the term at the worst possible time.

Connor glares at her. Ignatius stares at her. So do Shelby and Pip. Beads of sweat form under her feathers, and she becomes lightheaded.

"Open a what?" Connor barks.

"A...an...ugh. Account!" she suddenly remembers. "I wish to open a bank account with these anchovies," she stammers.

Connor takes one look at her sack of neatly folded bananas leaves and cackles. This time his facial expression cracks, and she thinks he's scarier than ever.

Connor's face turns cranberry red. He roars hysterically. In fact, he laughs so hard that he must brace himself on the kiosk counter.

Ignatius, on the other hand, doesn't laugh. But his reaction is somehow worse. Ripley sees Ignatius nodding, smirking, and shrugging in embarrassed agreement with Connor.

"Do you know where you are?" Connor bellows. "This is Her Majesty, The Queen's Imperial Piggy Bank. We don't deal in mere *dozens* of anchovies—"

"But these aren't dozens. I have a hundred and fifty anchovies here." Ripley hopes this will convince him.

"A hundred and forty-eight," Shelby corrects her.

Connor's face grows redder still, now in complete annoyance. "A hundred and forty-eight anchovies? Are you mad? We require a strict minimum amount to open an account here."

"What's a minimum?" Pip squeaks.

"It means they have standards. This bank only deals with wealthy individuals. You must have *at least* ten thousand anchovies to bank with them, love," says the emu passing by again. Once more, her spittle smacks Shelby in the face. And once more, her scent reminds Ripley of a spider monkey's armpit.

Connor continues nodding and wincing, as if to apologize to the other bank clients and to Connor. "My mistake," he says. "It's been a long time since I opened my first account. I forgot the rules and restrictions."

Connor snickers at the emu over Ignatius's head. "Next thing you know, this lot will want to invest with us."

"BWAHAHAHAHAH!"

The emu cracks up this time. So does Connor. Even previously reserved Ignatius breaks into a howl. All the animals at the bank begin to laugh out loud at Ripley, almost in unison.

The great commotion catches the attention of a group of even bigger, better dressed pigs who have been in a meeting behind the teller's desk. A conference room door opens, and a well-coifed bigwig inquires, "Hey, what's all the fuss out here?"

Through the glass conference room windows, Ripley can make out a presentation projected on the wall. At first, she notices a chart and then a jagged diagonal line. This line starts low in the bottom left-hand corner and shoots steeply to the right. She also notices the four letters "DNTR" in bold. What she doesn't have time (or sharp enough eyes) to read is the rest. DNTR Equity (Daintre e.com Inc.) M&A Deal—strictly confidential.

Any of this might as well have been Greek to her. And it might sound like nonsense to you, too, unless you're a financial guru already. Or maybe you're an investing savant.

Fist pumps either way, because that's where you're headed. You'll be a wizard in no time!

Still, two details have been seared into Ripley's mind: DNTR and that chart with the crazily shaped lightning bolt.

Almost unable to speak through his laughter, Connor pipes up. "Hey, boss. Get a load of this! These teeny, tiny, pre-teen penguins are inquiring about...hahaha...banking with us."

"Next thing you know they'll be interested in buying shares of Daintree. Bahhhahah!" More howls echo throughout the halls.

The boss responds from the door of the glass meeting room. "So sorry, littles. But that ship has sailed long ago. Fat chance you'll ever have enough to buy even one share of that company today. And what a pity it is, since that's what made us all mega-rich!"

"There was an element of luck sprinkled in, as is often the case when you directly invest in something so successful from an early stage. We must admit that. Investors didn't know then what we know now. No one truly could have anticipated how successful Daintree would become," says one bespectacled junior banker. But his colleagues don't seem to hear him. They keep talking over him.

"Yeah, Daintree turned most of us into billionaires, but we started investing decades ago. No way you could hang with us. But nice try!" The boss of the executive piggies truly delights in belittling the poor feathered wretches.

Humiliated, Ripley retreats. *What have I done? I miss home.*

With sunken shoulders and tears in her eyes, she slides down from the penguin tower that Shelby, Pip, and she had created. As she does so, she falls on her face. Slowly, she lifts herself up again, as she has done a thousand times before.

Down the hallway at a distance, she detects a different animal as it emerges from the conference room. She can't make out who or what it is. It's not a pig or hog, but it's somehow familiar. It couldn't be someone she knows. Could it? The animal's paws are hairy. *But...no,* she thinks. *Impossible.* After all, she's never been here before.

There's one last odd detail she notices about the vaguely familiar animal. Slung over its shoulder is a satchel emblazoned with the words *Blue Ventures.*

12

Sad Times for Terribly Sad Little Blue Penguins

Our little blue trio hangs its set of little blue heads.

With nowhere to turn, they waddle from the Piggy Bank. Sorry—they *trudge*. Here, too, trudge remains the ideal word to explain just how disappointed our group feels.

Their little blue eyes stay downcast. Even their flippers are limp. They're *almost* as sad as when they head to work.

"What do we do now?" Pip asks his big sister.

Ripley wishes he hadn't inquired. She's fresh out of answers and energy.

"We could eat some of the anchovies," Shelby offers.

"No! We're saving them to put in the bank. Remember?"

"Um...Ripley. The bank doesn't *want* our anchovies. The pigs turned us down. We're not rich enough. Remember?"

"Of course. My mistake, Shelby. And you're right. Some of the anchovies are starting to go bad. We had better eat those before they rot. But that's it. We save the rest." Ripley's still befuddled and confused. (IRL, when a dollar/anchovy today is worth more than a dollar/anchovy tomorrow, we call that inflation.)

As long as she lives, she'll never forget how that bully of a bank teller and his colleagues had laughed them right out the door. Nor will it ever slip her mind that the pompous emu and all the other animals had chuckled at their expense. Even Ignatius had thought her intentions had been a joke.

Pip stops his sad trudging momentarily to turn to the others. "Maybe we should go home now, you guys. It's getting late, and the trip will take hours without Rex."

Poor Pip. Ripley looks into his teary eyes. *I dragged him into this mess. It's been nothing but a nightmare. First, Rex died. Then Pip got trapped beneath him. What next?*

Fretting, Ripley slips into an emotional tailspin. Her feelings spiral out of control. She thinks about the other mess she had gotten her dad in, too. She recalls Banjo ordering Bork to brand her dad, punishment for a crime he hadn't committed.

Again, she feels the emotional weight. It's a heavy burden. And then, she thinks of Pip stuck under Rex. Followed by...Rex's death! *Oh, poor, Rex.*

All this disappointment is too much for Ripley. She's dizzy. She thinks she'll faint.

"Are you OK?" Shelby asks her. "You don't look so good."

Her head throbs. Her mouth is dry. *Really dry.* How dry? Imagine you were at the beach on a hot summer day. Sweating on top of your towel, you reach for a cold, refreshing bottle of water.

But it turns out somebody has played a cruel prank on you. They have replaced your water with sand. Thirsty, you gulp a bunch down before realizing the switcharoo. Can you imagine just how dry your mouth would feel after THAT?

That's how thirsty Ripley feels right now. She's parched, bone-dry from the inside out. And she thinks this world wasn't made for penguins like her.

Didn't we warn you that this corner of Australia was tinged with misery?

Just to clarify, the continent itself is tremendously lovely. There are heaps of things to see and do. Immense rainforests neighbor gorgeous coastlines and tide pools. Then there's the Great Barrier Reef, which speaks for itself. And, of course, who could resist the endless cafés with their delightful flat whites?

But back to Ripley and her devastating ordeal.

At this moment, she is M.I.S.E.R.A.B.L.E. Tired, hungry, and terribly thirsty, she wants nothing more than to be home—to call it quits on this whole misguided adventure. To say adios to banking and saving anchovies. Forever.

As such, coming across Rex's dead body doesn't cheer her up.

"Rex!"

In their misery, the sad little blue penguins had failed to notice that they'd wandered back to the spot where their cassowary had mysteriously met his demise.

Ripley runs over, hugging her stiff friend's bony, long legs with her outstretched flippers.

"Watch out!" Shelby leaps after her. "Whatever he got might kill you, too."

Even if that's true, Ripley doesn't care. She can't care. Too much has gone wrong. She doesn't have the headspace for a new worry.

To her surprise, Pip joins in beside her, hugging Rex with all his little blue might. "I don't care that you squished me. I believe you now, too, Rex. I'd take your advice. I didn't mean to push back so hard. Just stop being dead. Please," Pip sobs.

Of course, Rex remains motionless.

Ripley wants to cry with him, but she can't. Suddenly, she feels calm again, remembering that trying something, anything, is almost always the right path. She feels strong, and she needs to be. She needs to hold it together for Pip and Shelby. She stops hugging Rex and picks up Pip in a warm, gentle embrace.

When she looks up, she sees Shelby and gasps. "I didn't think you would try to eat all the anchovies, Shel. They're not *all* about to spoil."

"I'm not," says Shelby, an anchovy head clearly hanging from his mouth.

"I can *see* you. And that." Ripley points at Shelby's beak.

"Oh. Thith? This is just a little fish." *Gulp.* "One that I caught."

Ripley's eyes narrow angrily. "Oh, yeah? When?" And then she lets out a chuckle.

"While you two were hugging it out with Rex. Just now."

"Just now?"

"Yeah, I didn't want to disturb you, so I slipped away, dived into the ocean over yonder a ways, and caught me another fish to eat. If I had to guess, I'd say this is, er, a young sardine."

"Stop lying," says Pip, his eyes dry. "You stole that from Ripley."

"Did not."

"Did too!"

"If you're telling the truth, let me just count how many anchovies I have left." Ripley reaches over to her anchovy stash in banana leaves.

Shelby moves to stop her. "Don't!"

She won't be stopped. She charges straight ahead. Shelby jumps on top of her, and they go rolling through the tall grasses, punching and kicking each other.

"Get offa me."

"You get offa me."

Then...

"AHHHHH!" Shelby looks at Ripley as they both tumble forward.

"AHHHHH!" Ripley shoots a scared look back at Shelby. Both shriek as they roll together like a snowball in winter.

Pip waddles downhill after them, but he can't keep up. They gather momentum and don't stop spinning until they reach the bottom of the slope. What they see next shocks them to the core.

"Koala Café," reads a neon pink-and-gold sign. It's so bright that it blinds the penguins, even in broad daylight.

"Do you see what I see? Is this for real, Shelby?" Ripley questions. "Or have I passed out?"

The sign for the Koala Café sits perched on top of a cozy pub. It has ornately carved wood paneling and large, colored lattice windows. (We're wondering who thought pink and gold went well with wood paneling, let alone mid-century vintage green and leaded glass. We mean, really? Is this like *Cheers* in Palm Springs or something? Our minds are blown. But whatevs. We're not the ones who designed this joint... OK, technically maybe we are. SMH.)

Blue-gray, round-leaved eucalyptus grows along each side of the bar and casts a cool shadow over the building. A bright, minty scent puts the penguins instantly at ease. Ripley inhales deeply and lets out a sigh. She feels calmer already.

"What're you guys doing—" Just catching up to them, Pip notices the pub that seems to have popped out of nowhere.

"C'mon. Let's get something to drink. We need a break," Ripley suggests in a subdued, exhausted tone, trying to forget the fight she just had with Shelby.

Pip and Shelby follow her to the door. "Wait up."

As Ripley opens the door, she notices that wall to wall, the pub is jam-packed with koalas. Koalas are everywhere. Koalas galore. Koalas sipping from coconuts at bar tables. Serious-looking koalas in suits and ties are conducting business meetings. Festive koalas are celebrating a friend's birthday with what appear to be presents wrapped in still more eucalyptus leaves, both the round and the long-leaved varieties.

Koalas also wait in line for the loo—that's Australian for bathroom. In the far-left corner, koala servers in little aprons are carrying heaping trays of food and drinks as they leave the kitchen.

And in the center of all the koala commotion, behind the main bar, stands a weathered koala bartender with thick sideburns. His smoky, gray eyes let you know he's not surprised by much.

He takes one brief look at the three little blue penguins and shakes his very round, very furry koala head. "Sorry, mates. No unaccompanied minors."

"Pardon me?" Ripley asks.

"I mean you can't come in without an adult."

"Oh," says Ripley. "We didn't realize. Can we just have one quick drink? We've had such a long day, and—"

But the bartender interrupts. "I truly wish I could accommodate, and I love the energy you young folks bring to a place like this. But I could lose my license and have to close up shop."

Oh, well. At least he was nice, Ripley thinks as she turns with Pip and Shelby and heads for the door. "I promise we'll catch a break, guys," she mutters softly to Pip and Shelby. "I just know we will!" Even Ripley is surprised by her sudden positivity. But what does she have to lose? Or maybe it's the scent of eucalyptus doing strange things to her.

13

Surprise

Another pair of older, darker koala eyes glares fiercely at Ripley, Shelby, and Pip from the side of the café. The other patrons have started to notice the penguins. Aside from being young, their blue feathers command a bit of attention from the koalas—more than Ripley would like.

"Hugo, get them out of here!" A cute female koala, with a red bandana tied in a knot at her forehead, motions to the bartender. "The inspector was just here yesterday." Her eyes dart nervously from Hugo to the other guests. Another inspector could be here, at this very moment, disguised.

"All right, Willow." Hugo moves from behind the bar to escort the penguins. He shields them from the unwanted attention they now receive from guests throughout the tavern.

He growls loudly at the little blue penguins so his customers can overhear. "Don't come back without an adult!"

"Sorry about that, guys. I had to put on a bit of a show. Some of our guests don't like kids as much as Willow and I do. Occasionally, we even get an undercover cop in here who would just love to see us go under." He pauses. "Or is it down under? No, in Australia we're technically already down under. So just under. Oh, you know what I mean. But if you're ever back in town, specifically with your parents, please return. We'll make it up to you." With that, he ruffles Shelby's head feathers.

"Fat chance of that," Shelby mutters, as the café door closes behind them. "I'll never come back to this place. I'm done with long journeys and Piggy Banks and Koala Cafés."

But Ripley remembers her mom's advice: *Be the salmon*.

Ripley knows she won't be able to return with her parents. Her dad couldn't make the trek. But still she thinks this can't be the end of their adventure. She must keep swimming. She must swim upstream! Maybe this is what her mom had prepped her for all along.

Also, she's super thirsty and could use a nice cold drink from the Koala Café.

"What if we came back with a different grown-up?" Ripley asks suddenly.

Shelby and Pip can't believe their ears.

"What grown-up?" Shelby responds in confusion.

By now, Shelby is backing away from Ripley. He does *not* want to be the salmon. He wants to live to eat more salmon someday.

Little does he know Ripley has a plan. An insane plan. "Our friend Rex is a grown-up. He's practically standing right by that tree.

"But Rex is dead," Pip reminds Ripley.

Ripley doesn't want to hear him. She rushes back to the door of the Koala Café where Hugo still stands. He's been watching them from inside the tavern.

Ripley opens the door and from the entrance yells, "Can we come back with an adult who's not our parent?"

Curious nearby koalas at the bar look to Hugo for his answer.

"Sure thing. But everyone needs to order something."

"Of course," Ripley says. "Our friend's thirsty, too."

Twenty minutes later, three sweaty little blue penguins return to the pub. If you thought that Hugo had looked at them with wide eyes before, his koala peepers practically fall out of his skull this time.

Ripley, Shelby, and Pip have managed to lower Rex into a wheelchair that they found outside the café. Shelby pushes the chair slowly from behind, standing barely an inch taller than the radius of a wheel. He's able to see hundreds of koala feet and the ground immediately in front of him. But not much else.

Ripley sits up straight on the right side of Rex's lap. The cassowary's long legs are bent, crisscross applesauce. His round belly juts forward as though he'd swallowed a beach ball. Dark, thick-rimmed sunglasses shield his eyes.

Pip stands on Rex's slumped shoulder, struggling with all his might to keep the big bird's bright head from falling over.

"Of all the crazy things to do..." Shelby mutters under his breath.

"This will never work," Pip whispers to Ripley. "Abort. Abort!"

Ripley will not abort. She commands them onward by sheer will.

She plasters on a fake smile for Hugo as they parade Rex in his wheelchair through the bar.

"We are so busted," Shelby quivers. "They're going to arrest us, and we'll never get home. I don't want to know what jail's like."

Ripley keeps up her nervous, fake smile. "Just keep pushing. Pushing, pushing. We got this."

But do they? It's not so easy to scoot a massive, slumping cassowary across a koala pub floor. This is especially true when the animals doing all the shoving, lifting, and propping are three little blue penguins—creatures one fifth the height of their dead companion.

"This is the worst day of my life," Shelby pants as he presses on. "The..." *Huff. Huff.* "Worst."

"This will never work," Pip mumbles again, scared out of his mind.

Every single koala eye in the pub is fixed on Rex and his crew. Now Rex's chair moves just an inch at a time. One shove. Stop. Then another push. Stop.

"Just keep pushing," Ripley assures Shelby. "You're doing great. We're almost to the bar."

Somehow, they do it. The chair bumps into the bar with a thud.

They really did it.

Defying all odds, the three little blue penguins somehow managed to get Rex to the bar. Shelby looks at Ripley and Pip in elation.

"I'm hecka strong!" Shelby exclaims.

"Yeah, you are!" Ripley high fives with her flipper.

But then, Pip accidentally drops Rex's head. The cassowary's body starts to slide forward in his seat. His legs are stuck at his sides. And then...

Rex somersaults on to the floor. It sounds like a wet mop just slapped into the wall. All the koalas pull back with a gasp.

"Are you all right?" a concerned koala on a barstool asks Rex.

Busted, thinks Shelby. *So busted.*

Ripley thinks fast and scurries toward Rex's head. "He's fine. Rex falls down all the time. That's just his party trick."

To prove it, she drops Rex's head again, making the whole bar rattle like there's been an earthquake. "You stop that, Rex! You big kidder."

A few koalas burst into laughter.

"A flopping cassowary. Good one!" shouts another. "Don't see that every day now. Do you?"

"Have. You. Lost. Your. Miiind?" Shelby says to Ripley quietly.

"This will never work," Pip whispers for what feels like the hundredth time today.

Ripley turns to respond to the concerned koala. "Could you possibly assist? He's had a long day."

"Um, OK." The kind koala helps Ripley, Shelby, and Pip hoist Rex back into his wheelchair. Pip cautiously lowers Rex's head onto the counter.

"Four iced teas, please," Ripley calls out to Hugo, keeping up her fake smile.

Hugo doesn't budge. "What's wrong with your friend?"

Ripley climbs onto the stool beside Rex, straightening his sunglasses. "Oh, nothing."

"He has sunglasses on. Inside," Hugo points out.

Ripley laughs him off. "Oh, *that*. His pupils are dilated. He just came from the optometrist."

"He doesn't look so good. In fact, he looks...dead."

Busted. Shelby is too scared to blink.

Pip squeaks out a toot.

Be the salmon, Ripley thinks to herself. "Sir." She continues smiling at Hugo. "I know you didn't mean it, but don't you think it's rude to make fun of someone for being different?"

The concerned-looking koala looks up from his newspaper at Hugo. "Little girl's got a point. It ain't polite to insult one's customers."

"I'm not making fun of him, Kent. I'm worried for him. He looks dead!"

Scared, Pip toots again. Only louder. The air around him smells like hard-boiled eggs.

Rex's head tilts back, and he slides to the ground with another crash.

"Let me help you, sir," says Kent, a concerned koala. He lifts Rex back onto his wheelchair. Again. Ripley props Rex up and pats him on the head.

"Had a cousin like your friend," Kent tells Ripley. "Could sleep through anything. One time he even passed out in a crocodile's mouth."

"Did he turn out okay?" Ripley asks.

"Not that time. Crocodile ate him. But he was a heavy sleeper in general."

Hugo's heard enough. He slaps the bar. "I'm going to call an ambulance. Someone needs to check on him. A doctor."

"But you haven't brought them their iced teas yet."

Hugo glares at Kent. "You stay out of this. How would you kids even pay?"

"Wait."

They all turn to Shelby. "We have anchovies. We can pay you."

Shelby produces the four additional anchovies he stole from Ripley's stash, anchovies he planned on eating alone when she and Pip weren't looking.

Despite himself, Hugo stares. "Where'd you get those?"

"They belong to Rex," Pip speaks up. "He likes us to pay for him."

"Sounds like my other cousin," says Kent. "Also eaten by a crocodile."

Hugo reaches for the anchovies, then stops himself. "Let me get this straight. Your friend who hasn't spoken a word and looks dead, or at the very least heavily intoxicated, just likes to fall down?"

"Yes!" says Ripley.

"Your friend is possibly also so sleepy he must keep his eyes shut inside our bar?"

"Yes!" says Pip.

"And for some reason this friend also likes for you to buy his drinks?"

"Yes!" says Shelby.

"Okay, then," says Hugo. "You've convinced me. Four iced teas coming up. But if he doesn't improve, I'm calling emergency services."

With that, Rex falls out of his wheelchair again.

14

Weak-end with Rex

Hugo glares at Ripley. "Your friend's dead. Just be straight with me."

"Oh, he's just sleepy," Ripley assures him.

Hugo's skepticism has returned. "I don't serve unconscious or dead animals."

Ripley tries to win Hugo back with a smile. It doesn't work. Meanwhile, Pip and Shelby try their best to hold the cassowary up, but their energy is fading.

It's hard work. Super hard.

As you recall, Rex is massively heavy, and the little blue penguins can barely prevent him from crashing to the ground. Each time he plummets, Rex shakes the pub something terrible. We're guessing his last fall caused a magnitude 4.3 earthquake—not quite strong enough to topple the building. But it was definitely powerful enough to shake a few glasses from the bar's shelves.

Even Kent, that nice koala sitting beside them at the bar, has become suspicious of Rex's strange behavior. "Isn't your mate going to drink his iced tea? Why are his eyes still closed?"

Something else catches Ripley's attention. Behind Hugo, she eyes a TV. On it, an energetic newscaster talks fast, frantically waving his hands. Almost in a panic, he looks nervous. The bottom of the screen lights up red with a banner of text: *BREAKING NEWS: Daintree Stock Tanks.*

"Could you turn up the sound on that, please?" Ripley asks Hugo, motioning to the screen.

"Let's not avoid talking about our current conundrum, shall we?" Hugo replies. But he pivots nonetheless, and when he does, he's surprised by the news as well. He grabs the remote and cranks up the volume.

The newscaster is calmer now. He touches his finger to the side of his head and listens to his producers through his earpiece. His eyes focus on the desk in front of him. When he looks back up at the camera, it's as though he's speaking directly to his audience—to Ripley and Hugo and everyone else watching his program.

> "Ladies and gentle-creatures. I'm afraid we have shocking financial news. Trade tensions have negatively impacted some businesses but none as drastically as Daintree. We can hardly believe it, but Daintree's stock is tanking. It's in free fall. Investors across the globe are panicked."

The newscaster pauses. As if personally accepting defeat, he starts speaking again, largely repeating his prior message.

> "Good afternoon again, folks. For those of you just joining us, Daintree, perhaps the largest global delivery company in the world, is hurting. Badly. Earnings are way down. The company's stock value has been slashed in half in mere hours. Shares continue to fall. Could this be the financial end for Daintree? For us all?"

Hugo turns away. His face is pale. "Ugh. I think I'll be sick. There goes my entire retirement account!" He bends over and vomits into a trash can.

"Well, that's a real shocker. But I guess you never see a black swan coming until its arrived," chimes in Kent. "You should have diversified your holdings, Hugo."

"Huh? Where? I don't see a black swan." Ripley responds. "Oh, Rex isn't a swan. He's a cassowary."

"Sorry, little one. No, this has nothing to do with your friend. Black swan is just a figure of speech, something we call an unexpectedly negative event, especially as it affects financial markets and stocks," Kent explains.

She's curious to understand more, especially about Daintree and its value. (Sidenote: Recall that the well-fed pigs had been so confident in their Daintree investments, just hours prior. Were they still so jolly after the latest news? What do you think?)

***

"Please, sir. Could we please have our iced teas?" Pip begs. "We're awfully thirsty." He knows the news is bad, but he's not terribly interested in it himself. How could he be when he's so parched?

Hugo mindlessly pours four glasses of iced tea and pushes them across the bar. His eyes have glazed over, as if he's sleepwalking through a nightmare.

"Where were we? Oh, yes. Right. Sorry, bud. A bit of devastating financial news is all. Didn't mean to forget about you lot." Luckily for Rex, Hugo's concern for him has disappeared.

"Good thing we didn't invest, though. Right, Ripley?" Pip asks. "It seems like a lot of people lost a lot of money today and very quickly!"

"You just might be right, Pip." And for the first time all day, she truly feels relief. Maybe Shelby and Pip were correct all along. Investing could certainly be very risky. She just wants to have a quick sip of tea and get home.

15
Dead Man's Drink

Ripley shares a look with Shelby and Pip. Holding up Rex is hard enough. *How can they possibly make it seem like he's drinking iced tea, too?*

"Sure," Ripley blurts out. "Rex loves iced tea. Don't you, Rex?"

"Yes, iced tea is delish."

"He didn't say that." Hugo points from Rex to Pip. "He did."

This is true. Pip has thrown his voice, pretending to be Rex. He's pretending poorly.

Hugo's dour face has grown more serious, his brow furrowing. He's losing patience. A vein bulges in his neck.

"If he loves it so much, why doesn't he drink his entire glass?"

"The big guy's still sitting there with his eyes closed," Kent adds.

Normally, it's impossible for little blue penguins to look pale. They have feathers over their skin, after all. But Pip and Shelby are so scared, even their feathers begin to turn white.

Things *still* aren't getting better for Ripley.

Hugo stares at her. Kent stares at her. More customers look her way. She must do something.

Nothing comes to mind. Zilch. *Zero.* She's drawing a blank.

This should freak Ripley out. But then she hears koalas talking behind her. They're steeped in conversation that distracts her again.

"What's the point of only letting rich animals invest with us? Anyone should be allowed to invest. I say, the more animals who participate, the bigger the pot for everyone."

They just said the magic word. Or did they? Yes. Yes, they did. Invest!

Ripley whips around to see who's talking. Her eyes land on three koalas wearing polka dot suspenders and white collared shirts.

Bankers, Ripley thinks. *Koala bankers.*

Before Ripley can do anything, Hugo slams his fuzzy paw on the bar. "OK. Your weird friend needs to go. NOW."

Pip stares at Ripley wide-eyed. So does Shelby.

"Busted," he whispers.

Ripley won't admit defeat.

She has another crazy idea. "Rex, have some of your yummy iced tea." She slips her flipper around Rex's neck, so Hugo can't see what she's doing.

Pip knows her idea. And he *hates* it. He shakes his head. So does Shelby.

Ripley ignores them. *I'll just lower Rex's head, ever so slightly, so it looks like he's actually drinking*, she thinks.

She holds her breath, concentrating.

Don't drop his head. Don't drop him.

But she drops his head. His beak splashes into the iced tea.

"Now *that* was a satisfying nap. Bit on the long side, though, if I'm being totally frank."

Ripley, Shelby, and Pip's eyes go wide. Falling into his iced tea woke Rex! Cold wetness dripping from his beak, he cracks his neck, gargles for a good fifteen seconds, then stretches out his broad cassowary wings. They're so big they extend all the way to Kent and tickle the koala's nose.

"Terribly sorry about that, my good fellow," says Rex to Kent. "Wait. Who are you? And what the devil are we doing in this...quaint establishment?"

"You're alive!" Ripley throws her arms around him. So does Pip.

Rex turns to his little feathered friends. "Little Blue and friends! Jolly good drink, thanks." He leans toward them and whispers out of the right side of his beak. "Where are we?"

Shelby is too concerned about the koalas' perception to respond to Rex right away.

"See? Told you!" Shelby points his finger at Hugo.

"OK. OK. My bad." Hugo raises his hands in stupefied surrender and wanders off.

Rex pushes up his sunglasses and takes another sip from his iced tea before clearing his throat. Now he's the one trying to save face. "If I recall correctly, we were having a spirited discussion about investing. I was making the point that the more anchovies one saves and invests, the better off one could be. Perhaps certain creatures could even escape the torture of terrible tyrants, like..."

Ripley doesn't register any of this. She's still in shock. "Where'd you go?"

"Go?"

"You've been like...dead," says Shelby, covering his mouth.

"And you fell on me," says Pip. "I was trapped under you. You didn't smell that great."

"You were? How embarrassing. Next time I fall on you, kindly ask me to move. I will be most obliged. Honestly, it's no inconvenience. Happy to do it."

Rex covers his mouth and leans toward Pip. "Apologies for the gas. Was it really that bad?"

Pip nods his head vigorously. "Really, really bad."

"We all thought you were dead," Ripley exclaims, in an exasperated whisper.

"Even I," says Kent eavesdropping on their conversation.

"Oh, the whole death thing." Rex gargles again for another weird fifteen seconds. "Should've mentioned it earlier—my naps can sometimes run long."

"*That* was a nap?"

"Yes, a *cassowary nap*, if you will. The term doesn't roll off the tongue quite like catnap does. Some bright creature once suggested *cassnap,* but wouldn't that make others think I couldn't pronounce cat?"

Ripley, Shelby, and Pip say nothing. They're still too amazed Rex is alive.

Kent pipes up. "Cassowary nap." He pauses. "You're right. It doesn't have the same punch as catnap. I like the ring of cassnap, though, chap. I say, use it!"

"What are you even talking about?" Ripley blurts out in a muffled whisper. "We thought you were dead, Rex! We were all alone in the middle of nowhere. And then, we went with this wallaby named Ignatius to the Piggy Bank—"

"Oh! So you found it. Delightful."

"It *wasn't* delightful. It was *awful.* Everyone was rude there, especially a pig named Connor. He was a teller, and he laughed straight in our faces."

"No? He did?"

"Yes. Yes, he did. He told us we didn't have enough anchovies to bank there."

"Oh, right. They do require a minimum number of anchovies. Must've forgotten about that part. Sorry."

"You *forgot* that part? Connor made us feel so stupid. And so did a vile emu and the more senior piggy bankers. The whole lot. Plus, we were so thirsty and so tired by the end, and we had no idea what to do once we left."

Rex can see how bewildered Ripley is. He realizes everything has fallen on her little blue shoulders. (Penguin shoulders are extremely narrow, we might add. Nature designed them as an adaptation that allows them to "fly" through the water, as you surely know by now. But broad, these shoulders are not.)

In all literal seriousness, Ripley has had to do so much alone, despite Rex's wanting to show them the path. He looks in her eyes. "It wasn't supposed to go this way. It's just that...well, I have low blood sugar."

Ripley doesn't know what to say to that.

"That's why I take so many cassnaps. I don't like to admit it, but I'm getting older."

A mix of emotions rushes through Ripley. Most of all she feels relief. True relief. She thinks she will cry, she's so happy to have Rex back. But she stops herself. "We're just glad you're alive."

For the second time that day, she hugs Rex. He hugs her back. Then he says, "Guess this was a bust. No more banking in your future. Or investing. Oh, well. Freedom's a bit overrated anyway, I suppose. We best be getting back to your life of horrible misery in the burrow."

"Rex! We just heard something about investing and Daintree. Its stock is tanking," offers Shelby. "Whatever that means. But I think we dodged a bullet. This just proves investing isn't for us. What a silver lining!"

Rex gasps and appears as though he could faint again. "No. Truly? How? What happened? I need to hear more." Rex proceeds shakily to the exit.

Ripley doesn't follow him. Instead, she heads for the table with the koala bankers who had been discussing investing.

16

One Door Closes, Another One Opens

Ripley stops in front of the koala bankers with their polka dot suspenders. "I heard you say you're looking for animals to invest with you."

"You were spying on us?" asks the first banker, aghast.

"That sounds like Kent's doing," says the second banker, annoyed.

"He's *always* eavesdropping," says the third banker, alarmed.

"Yes, I am," calls Kent from across the bar.

"I didn't *mean* to listen in," says Ripley. "It's just that we've been traveling so far...in search of a bank and—"

"And just who are you, little girl?" asks the third banker.

Ripley introduces herself, Pip, and Shelby. She motions toward Rex at the door.

"Splendid. Name's Gerald." He offers his paw. "We're bankers, as you already guessed."

"Rex told us all about the magic of investing and personal finance. If it's OK, I have some anchovies here that I'd love to—"

"CLOSING TIME!" shouts Hugo. "Time to finish your drinks and go."

The koalas get up to leave and start walking in lockstep for the exit, including the three bankers.

Ripley is confused. "Wait. This watering hole is closing *already*?"

Gerald heads for the exit. "We koalas sleep eighteen to twenty-two hours a day, you know. That means we must pack in a lot during the hours we are awake."

"Is your bank still open?" Ripley asks, following after him.

Gerald chuckles. "Of course not."

Her face falls. "I see."

"It'll open when we get there. And then it closes when we leave. We also have a sophisticated online platform where our current customers can manage most of their banking needs themselves. But I recommend an in-person visit first."

Ripley sighs with relief.

"Drop in whenever you'd like today, young lady," Gerald adds. "In ten minutes, we will be open for a good twenty."

"Twenty minutes?" Rex asks. "That's all?"

"Oh. You'd be surprised. We can get a lot done in twenty minutes."

"Wait, where's your bank?" Ripley yells after them.

"It's at 11 South Wallaby Street," replies Gerald.

"Wallaby Street? Really? We were just there," Ripley says to herself, a bit confused.

"Perfect. Then you know where to find us." Gerald nods at Ripley with a smile and shoots out the door.

***

What's one good thing about koala banks? They don't have long lines. Sure, koalas might look sleepy after all the tranquilizing eucalyptus leaves they consume, but when they're awake, they're surprisingly efficient. You might be, too, if you rested twenty-two hours per day.

For these koalas, every second is crunch time. They squeeze in all the work a regular banker might put into an eight-hour day—into twenty minutes.

When you go to a koala bank it feels like life whizzes past. Even the guards outside—crocodiles, not kangaroos—talk lightning fast.

"Where are you going?" says the scary-looking croc who's blocking the entrance. His cold, expressionless eyes don't blink. A scar runs down his square cheek.

"We're here to—"

The swift-moving crocodile cuts Ripley off. "Fine. Keep it moving."

Once approved by the crocs, a coastal taipan (an extremely dangerous snake) scans the penguins' eyes. This is a part of this bank's highly sophisticated two-factor authentication (for established clients), and it serves as a background check for new customers. The taipan lets everyone enter the bank and conduct their business with the koalas.

"They really do move quickly here," says Rex, impressed.

Unlike the piggy bankers, koala bankers deliver a more personalized touch, too. No lines. No tellers. Each animal who enters is greeted by a fast-talking, fast-walking koala in suspenders who whisks you away into a small private room. Posh photos of eucalyptus trees in bamboo frames line the walls. The vibe is simultaneously modern and minimalist.

To their surprise, the suspenders-wearing koala who ushered Ripley, Rex, Pip, and Shelby into his office is none other than...Hugo.

"*You?*" Ripley asks. "You're our banker?"

"Well, whom were you expecting?"

"Maybe one of the koala bankers from the café? Not sure. I mean...just not...*you*."

"Noted. Now that we have gotten that insult out of the way, what brings you to the Koala Bank?"

Rex stops him. "Hold on. You're both a bartender *and* a banker?"

"Yes, I also enjoy quilting and selling my wares. Now, unless you'd like to talk more about me, I suggest we get down to business. We close in eighteen minutes and thirty-three seconds. Thirty-two, thirty-one..."

"Please stop that. I can't think," says Ripley. "You're acting strangely."

Shelby whispers to Pip. "How can he switch his personality so quickly? I thought he said he would take care of us at the bar. Didn't we leave on good terms with him?"

"I heard that," says Hugo. "And you're right, young lady. Where are my manners. I sometimes feel pressured to be productive here. It's a different energy from the bar."

"No worries. It's understandable. You wear many hats." Ripley proceeds with her business. She lays out all her anchovies in the banana leaves. "There are a hundred and forty-five-ish here. I had more this morning, but..."

Hugo's eyes narrow. "Where did you find all these?"

"I fished them," she corrects. "And then I wrapped and preserved them. I saved them." Ripley responds.

"And you want to know if you can deposit these here, in our bank?" Hugo asks.

Ripley nods nervously.

"It's quite enough for a savings account. Might I say, I'm impressed, young lady. Remind me of your name again, please?"

"Ripley," Ripley says, holding out her hand to shake his. "And this is my brother Pip. My best friend Shelby. And Rex." Ripley motions to each companion as she introduces them.

"Pleased to meet you all again. Full of surprises today, aren't you, my dear?" Hugo comments.

"I suppose."

"Please don't misunderstand. I'm just speechless because of what you've managed to accomplish. This is quite a sizeable savings for such a young bird."

"Really? Thank you," Ripley responds humbly. "We just want to know if it's enough to bank with you. The Piggy Bank turned us away and made us feel awful. But then, I overheard your colleagues saying that the Koala Banks are starting to take an interest in less valuable clients, like us."

"One hundred percent. Indeed. You have come to the right place. We think all our clients are valuable, regardless of where they find themselves on their financial journeys. Besides, we all must start somewhere, right? We would be honored to have you as our client." Hugo responds respectfully.

"Please just give me a moment to pull up the required paperwork to open a savings account for you."

"Thank you." Ripley grins. She can barely believe her ears. It IS possible for her to bank, just like Rex had told her.

But then she turns to Rex. "Wait. Do we want a savings account?"

"Why are you asking him?" Hugo asks.

"He knows these things better than I do."

"You can ask me, too. I'm now your personal banker," Hugo replies.

Ripley still doesn't fully trust him. But Rex nods that it's OK to proceed.

"If I put all my anchovies in a savings account, will it still be my money?"

Hugo lets out a chuckle. "Why wouldn't it be? Yes, my dear. It will remain your money. We will simply help you protect it."

Ripley breathes a sigh of relief and smiles at Rex. He was right after all.

"In fact," Hugo continues, "our savings accounts are also insured by the KDIC, or the Koala Deposit Insurance Corporation. The US has something similar for humans called the FDIC. Basically, anything you deposit with us up to two hundred and fifty thousand anchovies (or $250,000) is guaranteed by the government."

Hugo is the opposite of Connor. She can hardly believe it. How can tellers at two banks behave so differently toward their clients?

"Just to be completely clear, I can come get my money whenever I'd like?" Ripley asks.

"Yes, it *will* still be your money," he tells Ripley. "Think of it like parking your anchovies here. You can drive them home anytime you like. During banking hours, that is."

"You mean banking minutes," Shelby jokes.

Hugo starts to reply with a joke but doesn't want to make the penguins uneasy. "Yes, young man. During banking *minutes*." Hugo smiles warmly.

"Can I ask you another question?" Ripley asks.

"You just did—" Hugo sees Rex. "Sorry. Jokes and sarcasm are kind of my thing."

"They're still learning," Rex says. "Thanks for your patience and help."

Ripley smiles to herself. *It's good to have Rex back.* She asks her next question: "What's in it for the bank to hold onto my anchovies?"

Hugo would love to continue, but he looks at the clock and realizes there are only seventeen minutes left to close. "Unfortunately, we really don't have time for *all* these questions today. I have a few other customers to attend to—"

"Those customers will just have to wait," says Rex.

Hugo folds his arms. "You know, I have a button under my paw. If I press it, that crocodile you met outside will come running." The young penguins don't bother him, but Hugo remains skeptical of this oversized, flightless bird. He'd acted so oddly in the café but moments ago.

Rex straightens his neck and puffs out his chest at Hugo. Ripley has never seen him assume such a menacing stance. "Yes, but you'll be quite deceased before that crocodile ever breaches these walls." Rex turns to Ripley. "Please proceed, Little Blue."

Hugo gulps, hoping the cassowary will calm down. "What was your question again, Ripley?"

"Why would your bank want to help me protect my anchovies?"

"We're no charity, if that's what you mean. We charge a few small fees here and there. But more importantly, we, too, invest that money. Sometimes we loan it out and charge interest, for example."

There's that word again. Invest. And another one. Interest.

Ripley's eyes light up. She smiles at Rex, then back at Hugo. "And if I'd like to invest, sir. How might I do that?"

17

This Banking Thing Sure Isn't Easy

"Glad you want to invest with us," says Hugo. "Let's cut to the chase."

That's still no way to treat a bank customer. Even cassowaries know that.

"Apologies for my abruptness, Ripley. It's just that we're running out of time, and I might doze off the way your pal Rex claims he did in the café. So unless we get some of this cleared up in a jiffy, we won't get a chance to open your account today," Hugo explains.

Before Ripley can hand over her anchovies, Rex interrupts. "Wait." He stares down at Hugo. "Shouldn't you first explain to the girl her options?"

Hugo exhales at Rex. "What options?" Hugo realizes there's no way he'll get out of here on time.

"What options?" Rex points to the clock on the wall. "My good fellow, just because you wish to help the next customer before your crazy bank closes in the next sixteen minutes—"

"Fifteen minutes."

"Fine. *Fifteen minutes.* Just because koalas must squeeze everything normal animals do over the course of a day into a few minutes, doesn't mean you should rush Ripley. She needs to know her options before she decides if she wants to bank here—"

"But I *do* want to bank here," Ripley whispers to Rex. "I really do."

"It's our only choice," Shelby whispers. "The pigs turned us down."

"Fine. But don't let Hugo hear you say that," Rex shoots back.

"Um...I just heard everything you said. I'm sitting right next to you."

"Everything?" asks Rex. "Did you hear my tummy rumble, too?"

"Yes."

That makes sense. Koalas do have excellent hearing. Plus, Rex hasn't eaten in more than twelve hours. Right now, his tummy sounds more growly than rumbly.

Ripley doesn't want to think about bodily noises or functions right now. She needs to know her financial options. And fast. A vision of her dad branded with a "T" reminds her that she must protect and grow her anchovies. For him. And for her fellow blue penguins.

Otherwise?

She and her friends will *always* work for Banjo. They will remain his minions. Forever.

"What are my options?" She blurts out.

"Option one," says Hugo. "You put your anchovies into a savings account."

"Will that grow me more anchovies?"

"Yes," says Hugo. "It will grow your anchovies."

Ripley pictures anchovies popping out of the ground like flowers. "How much?"

"If you put all one hundred and forty-five of your anchovies into a savings account today, in two years you can expect to have an additional 14.86 anchovies. Our interest rate is currently very generous at 5 percent. And as with most investments, we offer compound interest, meaning you will earn interest on the interest!

"And," Hugo continues, "the longer you leave your money in the savings account, the more you benefit from compound interest. The interest grows exponentially (i.e., compounds) with time. That's what I call pure magic. And you never risk losing an anchovy in the process—unless, of course, you spend it."

"Almost fifteen extra anchovies? In two years? That's not bad. It could definitely help my dad."

Pip and Shelby shake their heads. "That's impressive. But it won't buy our freedom from Banjo."

"On the bright side, in twenty years' time, you'd have 384.73 anchovies," Hugo adds.

"But twenty years?!" Ripley shouts. "We'll all be dead. We aren't humans! I do like those numbers, though."

"Also, I feel like 384.73 might not make me as happy in twenty years as a hundred and forty-five would right now," adds Shelby, trying to sound mature.

"Maybe give Ripley another option," Rex suggests.

"Okay. How about buying a CD with your anchovies? That's another nice choice. There, too, you won't risk losing what you start with."

"What's a CD?" Ripley asks.

"Ummm. Well..."

"You don't know what a CD is?" Rex questions Hugo as well.

Hugo looks uncomfortable. "No. Of course I do. But I don't know that it would do much more for her than a savings account these days."

"He's a funny banker," Shelby mutters under his breath.

"I heard that."

Ripley turns to Rex. "Can you please explain what a CD is?"

"Certainly. A CD, or certificate of deposit, is like a savings account. But it guarantees you a fixed interest rate, and that interest also compounds—just like in a savings account. The interest rate might be slightly higher than in a savings account.

"But if you purchase a CD," Hugo says, "you agree to leave your money with a bank, like us, for a certain amount of time. If you have to take your money out sooner, you owe us a penalty."

"Ouch. I don't like penalties." Pip envisions being beaten by Banjo or his henchmen. "How long do you usually need to keep money in a CD?" asks Pip.

"Usually a few years. Let's say five, for good measure."

"Five years?" says Shelby. "That's a long time. I hope to have children by then."

"Right on—then it's back to a savings account. At least then you will be able to retrieve your anchovies whenever you desire. You can use them to bail out your dad, stuff your face occasionally, or maybe you'll want to pay for something you aren't expecting right now—like Taylor Swift concert tickets. Just remember, you won't earn interest on the fish you take out." Hugo counters.

"Even if I don't want to buy a CD right now, why would the bank sell one?" Ripley asks again, her curiosity in finance topics unwavering.

"Right," says Hugo. "Where was I? Oh, yes. If you buy a CD, it gives us (the bank) a better chance of investing ourselves. A CD is less risky for the bank because we know how long we will have access to our clients' money. Then, we can loan it out, for example, to someone who wants to build an outhouse or a set of public toilets."

"Seriously? Why in the name of Philipp's Island would someone want to do that?" Shelby asks.

"Well, maybe because they don't want to relieve themselves outside. Maybe they fancy a bit of privacy on the loo. It's all the rage these days," Hugo explains.

"I'm not buying it, Hugo," Shelby argues. "Seems like a lot of trouble for a private poo."

"You'd be surprised what wealthy animals will pay for these days!" Hugo chuckles. "I didn't believe it myself when I first heard. But I've seen these contraptions with my own eyes. But back to your earlier question," he continues. "The longer you commit to leaving your money with us, the better we can predict and plan for our own investments. That's where a CD comes in handy for us."

"OK... If you say so."

"So why is it better than a savings account for us?"

"CD's usually pay a bit better, and the interest rate is guaranteed. Interest rates on savings accounts can fluctuate. Sorry, chaps. I mean they can change—go up and down."

Ripley asks cautiously, "OK, so how much more would your CDs currently pay than the savings account?"

"Only a smidge—5.5 percent for five years." Hugo pulls out his koala calculator. His paw is surprisingly fuzzy, even for a koala's. He does the math. "If you bought a CD with all one hundred forty-five of your anchovies today...and you didn't touch them for five years...you would get precisely 44.51 more anchovies. Put differently, you would have a total of 189.51 anchovies in five years."

"That's not bad," says Ripley. "But we can't touch it for five years?"

"No, that would cost you half your anchovies—the penalty. At least."

"But no one would hit us?" Pip wonders in delighted surprise. "The penalty is just money?"

"Why, yes, dear boy. What did you expect? We're bankers, not barbarians," Hugo replies with a quizzical look. He wonders what other tortures these penguins must have endured, but he's too afraid to ask. Ripley takes a moment to think about her banking options, which are both impressive and clearly better than just keeping the stash in her burrow, where Onyx and Banjo could find them.

If only she hadn't learned of the slight chance—however slight it truly was—that the penguins might be able to buy their freedom from Banjo. Prior to today, she surely would have left her stash in the savings account or CD and been most pleased. Unfortunately, she now has her sights set on something bigger.

Ripley runs her flipper back and forth across the edge of her lower beak as her eyes dart between Shelby and Pip.

"Any thoughts or decisions, Ripley?" Hugo asks.

Ripley lowers her flipper to speak. "Yes, actually, Hugo." She turns to Rex.

"This wallaby we met. This guy with a briefcase. The one who took us to the Piggy Bank. His name was Ignatius. He's the one who helped us get Pip out from underneath you, too, Rex."

"Dreadfully sorry about that again, Pip," Rex apologizes to the penguins.

"That's OK, Rex," Pip replies. "We all survived!"

"Anyway, Ignatius and the pigs had said something about investing in a company. A company called Daintree."

Rex's eyes widen. "What do you know about Daintree?"

"Not much. Except I see signs for it all the time, on trucks and packages and billboards. And do you remember that turtle driver we passed on our way here? He drove a delivery truck for Daintree. They sell things. Like food and books. And clothes. They seem to be everywhere."

"And that." Pip points to Hugo's calculator. It has the Daintree logo on it.

Rex is impressed by the penguins' observations.

"Oh, boy. I can't recommend you invest in Daintree right now, my dear. I would highly discourage it. Weren't you with us when we got news that their stock tanked today? At the café? I could have sworn you heard about it," says Hugo.

Rex's smile turns to a frown. "Wait, what?" He only partially remembers what took place in the Koala Café after waking up. "What else did I miss? It can't be. That would mean..." Rex sinks to the floor, and his voice trails off.

"Yes, I was there, but I want to understand. Is that a bad thing?" Ripley won't give up. "Why shouldn't we invest, Hugo? It seems like a solid company, even if their stock is down...or whatever you just said."

"It's currently a dreadful investment, Ripley. People are losing money right and left. Good companies can struggle, too," Hugo says.

"But why? Why shouldn't I invest? When would be a good time?"

"There are real risks to investing in the stock market, especially in the short term," says Rex. "Big risks. You could lose everything."

Ripley gulps. "Everything?"

"Maybe you should tell her how the stock market works," says Hugo.

"Can't you, please?" asks Rex. He's still too shocked by news of Daintree's stock slide.

Five minutes to close, Hugo is exhausted and drifting in and out of sleep himself. "Can I pour my nice customers a bit more...iced tea?" His voice becomes muffled, and he rests his head on the counter.

***

"And he calls himself a banker?" Pip mutters to Shelby, as he points at the zonked-out koala.

Hugo overhears and perks up. "Hey! You try holding down two jobs and sleeping twenty-two hours a day."

Ignoring him, Rex turns to Ripley. "Here's how the stock market works. In a nutshell, imagine you had a huge pumpkin—"

"I have a pumpkin in a nutshell. Pumpkin. Yum. Got it," chuckles Shelby. "I love pumpkins, especially tiny ones that fit in nutshells."

"You don't even know what a pumpkin is," says Pip.

"So what? The word sounds delicious, and it's fun to say. Pumpkin."

"No, I don't mean there is an actual pumpkin in a nutshell. It's a figure of speech, Shelby."

Shelby chuckles.

"Moving on," says Rex. "Imagine that this pumpkin produced seeds that it could sell to make the pumpkin money. Then the pumpkin decided to sell off tiny, little slices of itself. Maybe it wanted to expand its pumpkin-growing business and needed extra money to do so.

"These slices would be called shares," Rex explains. "The original pumpkin could sell hundreds or thousands of these—shares of seed-producing pumpkin—to other animals. We call the other animals who buy shares investors. And each share would have a certain value."

Ripley is trying her best to follow along. "A value? Can I take my shares home with me?"

"Yes and no. Yes, each tiny pumpkin share could be bought and sold for money, which gives it its value. But no, you couldn't take the shares home. The pumpkin can only produce seeds, if it stays together. You would own the rights to the pieces of pumpkin, though. In fact, investors technically would own part of the pumpkin itself. But the pieces must stay together.

"Now, let's say each share or portion of pumpkin is worth ten anchovies today. The pumpkin has been healthy and is supposed to keep producing seeds quite well."

"Sounds good."

"In our example, ten anchovies is the price that lots and lots of investors (buyers and sellers) have agreed upon at this one point in time. That's what we call a price set by a market—a large collection of buyers and sellers.

"Now, here's the interesting part. Imagine if, suddenly, pumpkin seeds got really popular. Maybe initially not everyone knew about pumpkin seeds. As soon as they tasted them, however, they all fell in love—"

"I like them already," says Shelby, rubbing his tummy.

"Shh," says Pip.

"With its increase in popularity, the company would sell more and make more seeds and make more profit. Then, as more investors noticed, they might buy more shares (i.e., invest). Then your share of the pumpkin could go up in value, maybe even reaching a hundred anchovies in a relatively short time. Some stock prices can swing quite dramatically. This is especially the case for growth stocks and public companies like Daintree."

Shelby is practically drooling. "A hundred anchovies..."

"Quiet," says Pip.

"But the best and worst part? You probably wouldn't need to wait twenty years for a share of your pumpkin company to make you rich if you invested in the right company at the right time. BUT—and this is a huge but—"

"He said 'butt.'" Shelby laughs to Pip.

"No, he said 'huge butt!'" Pip jokes back.

"Yes, I did. And here I go again, little fellas. BIG BUT, the company's stock can, quite literally, end up in the potty. It can tank. That's what we just saw with Daintree."

Ripley can't believe her ears. This is a lot to take in. She can't understand how different investments can produce such different amounts of money. Most importantly, how has she never heard of all this before?

"Stocks it is, Ripley," Shelby exclaims. "I was a skeptic of this finance and investing stuff at first, but if I can have ten times the number of anchovies in a week, sign me up. You had me at one hundred, Rex."

"Not so fast," says Rex. "There is no guarantee. Remember the 'big butt' thing?"

"Plus, those are my anchovies, Shel," Ripley adds.

"I would recommend starting small and getting to know the companies you invest in first. Greed can make investors act very irrationally. They start making bad choices and mistakes," Rex says. "You see, investing in the stock market can cut both ways, as I just warned, especially in the short term. Make sure you've thought things through, and you fully understand what's at stake."

Shelby makes a dour, disappointed face.

"Let me ask: What do you think would happen if animals suddenly stopped liking pumpkins? Or, what if your pumpkin couldn't keep producing seeds? Or consider that there were suddenly so many pumpkins that animals got sick of pumpkin seeds—"

"I would never get sick of pumpkin or its seeds," says Shelby.

"Well, if lots of animals did, the value of your pumpkin could go down," Rex goes on. "Your stock could go from being worth ten anchovies to five. Or two. Or one."

Ripley's face falls. "We would be worse off than where we started. With nothing."

Rex nods in agreement. He then adds, "As far as stock investing is concerned, I suggest investing in index funds, over a long time period, so you can diversify (i.e., spread out) your risk, but that's another concept for another day."

Hugo nods. "That's why I typically recommend that little blue penguins do the safe thing and put their anchovies in savings accounts or CDs, where they won't risk losing the amount they start with."

"Have you had any other little blue penguins as customers?" Ripley asks Hugo.

"Technically, no. But that's what I would advise them to do. Slow and steady wins the race." He turns to Ripley. "My advice? Park your anchovies in an account with a decent interest rate and wait as long as you can. That way you won't lose anything, and you benefit from compound interest."

He's right, Ripley thinks sadly. *So much for buying our freedom. That might be too greedy.*

Shelby turns to Rex again. "So can we really buy part of that pumpkin?"

Rex ignores him.

Hugo turns to Ripley. "One minute left 'til closing time. What'll it be?"

A little voice inside Ripley's head keeps repeating: *Be the salmon. Be the salmon. Be the salmon. Be the...* Until the voice in her head blurts out "Be the salmon" for her companions to hear.

18

The Apple Doesn't Fall Far from the Tree. Or Whatever.

A contract etched on a boulder reads: "This blissful community of little blue penguins belongs to Banjo in exchange for his amazing protection. For this wonderful, super-nice gesture, all future little blue penguins agree to work with him. They will catch him a daily quota. The only way this contract may be broken is if, by some stroke of impossibility, the penguins pay Banjo a sum of five thousand anchovies."

This inscription is the first thing Ripley reads as she and her feathered friends return to their burrow-town. She can't miss it as she rides atop Rex with Pip and Shelby flanking her at her sides. At this point, you may be like: *Wait. Why are we talking about signs? What the heck did Ripley choose to do with all her anchovies?*

Good questions. Thank you for asking. You're in luck. We have answers.

Well, Ripley decided not to leave her anchovies at the bank after all.

"*What?*" Pip asked confusedly, as Ripley led them out of the Koala Bank, the one that only stays open for twenty minutes a day. Rewind to the end of the prior scene.

"Really? We came all this way," Shelby added.

Even Rex looked perplexed by Ripley's sudden change of heart.

But Ripley had good reason for her decision. "I'm going to give these anchovies to the other little blue penguins in our community."

Shelby did not like this idea. Not at all. "Why?"

Honestly, Ripley wasn't sure. She couldn't fully explain her choice. "It just feels, I don't know...selfish to hoard all these anchovies. The whole reason I saved them in the first place was to help my dad. But I've caused so much trouble, for everyone. All I want now is to share them with our friends and family back in the burrow. We all toil away so hard every day. I'd like to help them, to help you."

"Or," said Shelby, "we could play a really fun game. We could see who can stuff their face fastest with all hundred and forty-five anchovies. Quick. I'll get us going."

Ripley stopped him. "No, Shelby. Please don't," she said with a calm seriousness in her voice. "But you and Pip can have two each for all the trouble I put you through."

"Really? Thanks," said Pip.

"How about *three* each?" asked Shelby.

"Fine."

And so, after their fishy treat, Rex toted them back to the village, running as fast as his spindly cassowary legs could take them. They arrived just shy of nightfall, but unfortunately, he didn't get them home undetected. For as soon as he let them scoot down his back and bid them farewell, Onyx catches sight of the trio.

The seagull's eyes zero in on the sack of banana leaves resting on Ripley's shoulder. (Sidenote: Onyx almost never removes his shiny, chrome shades. In fact, he even wears his sunglasses at night so he can watch the penguins weave and keep track of them without their knowing.)

How can she possibly be in possession of all those anchovies—again? Onyx wonders. The sight makes his blood boil. "Well. Well. Well," says the seagull to himself, circling overhead. "Look who's back."

The little blue friends stumble upon the contract we described at the start of the chapter. Ripley kicks it with her webbed foot.

"What'd do you that for?" asks Pip.

"This sign makes me so angry." She reads it aloud: "'For this wonderful, super-nice gesture, all future penguins agree to work with him.' What a lie. We don't work *with* him. We work. No, we slave away *for* him. Plus, what is he even protecting us from? Cassowaries aren't a threat."

"Agreed. But what can we do about it?" asks Pip. "The grown-ups signed a contract with him before we were even born. We just realized there's basically no way to make it to five thousand anchovies with a savings account or a CD, at least not before we die. This is just our sad fate."

"He's right." Shelby shakes his head. "We just need to accept that we can't do anything to change our lives. We might as well go home and rest. Soon, it'll be time to get up again and return to our routine. Back to diving for more anchovies for Banjo. Hey, at least we still have our puke picnics."

Ripley knows he's right. Maybe they just need to enjoy what they can—be grateful. No need to be greedy.

She and Pip follow Shelby toward their burrows as the sun sinks behind the grassy hilltops. Fading specks of molten orange fuse with blackness as night replaces day. The trio stands at the center of the little blue penguin village. Inside their burrows, Ripley thinks of sweet penguin families nestling into their beds. In a few hours, when they awaken, their cycle will resume.

They will be back at it, laboring for Banjo. Wake, work, puke, sleep. Repeat.

"Well," says Shelby to Ripley and Pip. "It's been real. Thanks for an adventure of a lifetime."

"Not so fast!"

They look up to see a flurry of wings thrashing toward them. Onyx. Next, an army of Tasmanian devils swarms from all sides.

"Oh, no," Pip trembles. "Not tonight."

The commotion stirs the rest of the little blue penguins from their burrows. They gather outside to see what's happening. Ripley's face falls as she eyes her poor dad. He walks slowly toward them with a giant bandage on his shoulder.

Finally, Banjo emerges from the shadows.

His scruffy dingo face remains expressionless. Is he angry? Surprised? Constipated? It's unclear.

The animals watch anxiously to see what Banjo will do next. He wastes no time stalking toward Ripley. She's scared and exhausted but somehow unshaken. She's witnessed and experienced in a single day more than most little blue penguins could manage in a year.

"Would you mind?" he says in a surprisingly gentlemanly tone.

As Ripley obliges, he delicately removes the bundle of anchovies from her arms like he's taking a fragile robin's egg from a mama bird's nest.

Banjo sighs sadly. "What am I to do with you naughty crew?"

"You could return us to our homes." Shelby can't help himself.

"Shh," says Pip.

Banjo looks like he might seriously consider this option. He's had a long day, too. "But no. That won't do. You'll just run off again with even more of my anchovies."

"I could smash their faces," Bork, the Tasmanian devil, chimes in quickly, his voice still squeaky and high.

"Thank you for that helpful option," says Banjo.

"No problem at all, boss."

"As I was saying—"

"I have other ideas, too, boss. I could throw them off a mountaintop onto jagged rocks."

"Really great options. Thank you, Bork."

"Wait, boss. I have more. I could locate a den of poisonous rattlesnakes and then push them in it."

"That'll do. Thank you."

But Bork can't stop. "I know. How about this: I drop boulders on them until they're so smushed into the ground they're virtually invisible."

"Enough!" shouts Banjo.

"Sorry, boss."

Ripley's about to blank out. She knows she's lost all control. And then she looks over at her dad with his bandaged shoulder. He secretly flashes her a tiny, brave smile.

Salmon, she tells herself. *Be the salmon. This must be the moment Mom prepared me for. I AM the salmon.*

Ripley is so focused on repeating her mantra to herself, she doesn't notice Banjo's staring at her, the wheels of his evil mind turning. He pivots to face the village.

"Ripley has been bad. A very bad girl. But I am not surprised. As the saying goes, the apple doesn't fall far from the tree."

Ripley takes a deep breath and locks flippers with Pip, then Shelby.

"But I won't punish Ripley. That won't fix the problem." Banjo stares at the entire assembly of little blue penguins. "Instead, I'll punish all of you."

19

It's Not Every Day You're in Danger of Falling to Your Death

Ripley looks around in horror. It's too awful to be true. But it is. Her fellow blue penguins are missing at least half of their feathers. Blue plumes lay scattered on the ground.

But this isn't their molting season, when the penguins should lose their feathers, allowing for new, healthy ones to regrow. No, this is the result of torture. Onyx, Bork, and Banjo's army have plucked the penguins ragged.

"You can thank the *other* traitor Ripley for your misfortune," Banjo proclaims.

Banjo and his terrible baddies turn to depart.

As Ripley looks out among her tormented friends and neighbors, all she sees are angry faces. Accusing faces. One, in particular, stands out. The angriest of all belongs to Indigo. She raises an exhausted flipper at Ripley. "You! You and your dad. How *could* you?"

Murmurs of weary agreement ripple through the furious crowd.

"Banish her!" someone says.

"Banish them *both*," says someone else. "She and her dad don't belong here. Nothing but trouble. Just like Sapphire."

With that, Nigel gets pushed toward Ripley. He reaches out to hug her.

"It's not your fault," he whispers.

"Oh, yes, it is," says someone else. "If only she did as she were told. Why must she always try to be so different?"

Ripley desperately scans the crowd, looking for Shelby and Pip. She could really use friends right now. And a time machine, if she's being honest. If only she could rewind the clock a few hours and tell herself: *Don't be the salmon. At least not now.*

She could have prevented this nightmare from ever happening.

But something more important is pressing. There's something worse than seeing all her fellow blue penguins looking raggedy.

"No!" her dad cries.

The whole village looks as though it's turned into a pack of zombies. They're a disillusioned crew, exhausted from experiencing such physical torture. They start swaying, moaning, and leaning on Ripley and Nigel, pushing them back and forth. Ripley's never seen her peaceful peers so disoriented and scary. It's as though someone has taken over their minds or eaten their brains.

Ripley sees where they're headed and gasps. They're leaning right for a cliff. Only a few feet separate her and her dad from the edge that towers high above a set of sea rocks and menacing waves.

Is this the end? she wonders.

Ripley toots. Nigel farts.

Pushed to our deaths?

Wow. This story got a *little* bit dark; didn't it?

Thankfully, you're not getting the full picture. Our sweet little blue penguins would never do something so awful as throw Ripley and Nigel off the cliff into the ocean. Sure, it's awful getting mutilated and having your little feathers pulled out by Banjo's goons. But the penguins would never do something so vicious to each other.

At least not on purpose.

You see, they're not possessed. They're just a scared colony. Fun fact: Colony is another name for a collective group of penguins. Another fun fact? A bunch of swimming penguins is called a raft. And a group of walking penguins?

That's a waddle. Seriously.

But we bet you're not interested in knowing these random facts at this precise moment. No, you probably want to know just what is going on with Ripley, Nigel, and the colony that appears ready to thrust our penguin friends to their deaths.

Nigel and Ripley have broken free, and they're running scared.

"Look," Nigel points.

Ripley sees it, too. Her whole rookery has retreated. *Why? Probably out of fear.* Can you remember what scares penguins the most?

If you happened to guess dirty diapers you're way off. That's not the answer, but we like the creativity. It's also not giant tarantulas. Although that would surely scare us. A lot.

No, the little blue penguin zombies back away in dread of their mortal enemy: the huge, massive, gigantic cassowary coming straight for them.

Plus, who or what is on top of this cassowary? Why, Pip and Shelby, of course. They're riding atop Rex, desperately calling for calm among the colony.

Only the colony doesn't listen.

The lot is too damaged, dehydrated, and depleted to think.

It's Ripley's turn to act. If she doesn't, she and her dad, and everyone she loves will fall off the cliff and plunge to their deaths.

It's too awful to imagine. So, let's not.

Ripley lets go of her dad's flipper and leaps high into the air (despite her short legs) as Rex approaches. She lands on top of the closest penguin, a grown-up by the name of Denim who happens to have quite bad breath. But Ripley doesn't have time to think about stinky, cheese-smelling breath right now. (Sidenote: It must be the stress. Did you know stress could produce bad breath? It even has a name: Halitosis.)

Sorry. Where were we? Oh, yes. Ripley must get to Rex before it's too late. She leaps from Denim's shoulder on to another grown-up named Leo, who has a distinctive, dark azure plume atop his head. From there she hops over Violet to Kai, then kneels on Orla—then over Cobalt, and finally to Marin.

Yes, in case you're wondering, these are real penguin names. Or, should we say, really cool real penguin names? Little blue penguins are clever on many fronts.

Finally, Ripley takes a flying leap onto Rex's helmet-like crest.

Except she misses. She ends up swaying from his wattle, which makes her bounce up and down like she's a ball pinging off a paddle. She poings and ricochets back and forth from the ground to the sky. It's so strange that the whole colony stops moving to marvel at the spectacle.

"Are you quite done now?" Rex whispers. "I wouldn't mind regaining control of my wattle. Thank you very much. Plus, everyone's staring at me, and you know how I loathe unwanted attention."

"Do I?" Ripley barely squeaks out. She wants to tell him that she's bouncing up and down not because she wants to be on rollercoaster, but because she's hanging on for dear life.

At last, she lets go and front flips to the ground.

"Are you okay, Little Blue?" Rex asks her.

The other little blue penguins can't believe their little blue ears. *A fearsome cassowary asking Ripley if* she's *OK*? *Acting like he knows her and using a nickname to boot?*

Rex helps her up, dusting her off. "I came just as soon as Pip and Shelby found me."

The other penguins are stunned. *Ripley really knows this beast?*

"We found him in the middle of another cassnap," Pip says to Ripley.

"A delightful one, too," adds Rex. "I dreamed I was the lead singer of a brilliant rock band. We were called the Coconuts. We even had amusing T-shirts made for our world tour. Let's see now. I think we were about to begin our opening act in Sydney. Or was it Melbourne...? Oh, definitely Melbourne. We were set to open for AC/DC."

As Rex tries to recall the details of his rock-star dream, the colony stares back at him in wonder. Okay, stupefaction. That's a big word meaning dazed and confused. Here's another. They are simply gobsmacked to see this cassowary, someone they thought was a cold-blooded killer, speak so casually with their fellow little blue penguins. He doesn't appear the monster they'd been told he was all these years.

Instead, he seems quite nice.

To prove it, Rex treads over to Nigel to inspect his injury. Without seeking approval, he peeks under the bandage and spits on Nigel's wound.

"Patooie!"

Then he carefully removes the covering. "No need for that any longer, my good fellow. Now," Rex turns back to Ripley. "Where were we?"

Shocked and stunned, Nigel moves his opposite flipper to touch the gash. But it's no longer there. The skin doesn't even hurt. Nigel peers down, and to his sheer amazement the sore has healed. A scar remains, but the injury has healed ever so nicely. (Sidenote: If Rex's spittle is more effective than antibiotic ointment, maybe we should market it. What do you say? Anyone for Cassowary Cream?)

20

Can We Be Salmon, Together?

Hours later, the colony huddles beneath Ripley's beloved magnolia tree. It's nighttime. Fireflies flit all around, lighting up the darkness around them like blinking flashlights on tiny helicopters.

Gone is the little blue penguins' fear of Rex.

The little blue penguins are no longer alarmed by cassowaries. It's amazing how quickly their minds have gone from fearing something to being...well, cool with it. Even though we're grown-ups writing this story, nighttime monsters still make us jump. That's why we insist on leaving the hall lights on when we go to sleep.

Kidding. Or are we? Best to face your fears...no?

Anyway, as you'll recall from Chapter 18, Ripley opted not to place her anchovy stash in the Koala Bank. (*Why did we even create this book?* you ask.) Instead, she surprised her best friend and little brother by deciding to share the extra anchovies with the rest of colony.

Except things didn't work out that way. That happens every now and then, right?

As you might expect, Banjo the Baddest Baddy gummed up Ripley's plan and stole her entire stash, again—the remaining 141 (or so) of the salty fish the little blue penguins love, Shelby most of all. (Sidenote: This number is an estimate. We can't be sure how many extras Shelby sneakily snuck from the stash.)

Remember him? Of course you do.

He did not like Ripley's idea at first. If he had had his way, we think he would've eaten the anchovies or invested quickly in a company he hadn't fully researched.

But all that doesn't matter a fig now.

Banjo and his goons have bested the little blue penguins. Not only is the whole colony missing countless beautiful feathers—Ripley has nothing to show for her efforts.

To put it another way, Ripley and friends are back at square one. And in a story like this, square one stinks. It's the pits. The worst.

Actually, being at square one isn't the worst. All the little blue penguins could be dead by now—killed in the dreadful manner Larry experienced, back in Chapter 2. So, yes, things could be worse.

But things are still not good. Not good at all.

So it makes perfect sense for Ripley to stand before the huddle that is currently gathered in her happy place to share her brilliant, new idea.

"Attention, everyone..." she says. "If I could please have your attention for just one second."

No one pays her any attention. None. Zero. Zilch. Can you blame them?

They are too busy doing the kinds of things little blue penguins do when they get together. Plus, they just escaped death and survived torture, so there's that. They gossip about recent events. Others waddle about in circles. Some pick their noses.

Again, Ripley tries to get their attention. "Excuse me, please..."

This time, Pip and Shelby look up at her. So does Rex. Until now he had been discussing the merits of cassnaps with a curious little blue penguin named Leo. Remember him from Ripley's parkour scene—the penguin with the dark blue feather? The segment where she jumped from penguin to penguin? Well, Leo also enjoys brief, refreshing siestas.

As for the rest of the colony? They don't notice Ripley is waving her flippers to get their attention. "Look here, please..." she pleads.

Seeing Ripley struggle so much, Rex decides to step in.

"Give me a second, please. Will you, Leo?"

Rex unfurls his massive cassowary wings. With his gargantuan wingspan the size of a luxury sports utility vehicle, all the penguin eyes immediately gravitate toward him.

"Oh, no," says Kai, the otherwise super-chill penguin. "He really is going to murder us. Waddle for your lives!"

Suddenly fearful again, the whole colony runs toward the cliff to their deaths. Kidding. Kidding again. That didn't happen. Also, that would be a terrible joke to play on all of you who have been most kind to read this far.

No, instead, they look up at Rex who points to his dear friend. "Ripley has something she'd like to share. Take it away, Little Blue."

With the colony's attention fixed on Ripley, she begins to tremble. Have you ever had to stand in front of your class to give a book report? Maybe you've done a math problem on the board? Did it make you nervous? That's how Ripley feels now. Suddenly the center of attention, Ripley is shy.

The power of speech fails her.

"Um, sis? They're waiting for you to say something," Pip whispers.

"Anything," adds Shelby. "It's getting weird."

Ripley senses the awkward pause as she stares out into the crowd, her eyes fix on the little blue penguins she grew up with: Indigo, the wise elder, Perry, the scaredy, Kai, the dude the other kids look up to. At last, her eyes settle on her dad.

Nigel smiles at her as if to say: *You got this.*

Ripley takes a deep breath. She never hoped to be a hero. That was not her plan. She only wanted to help her dad. And that had required her to follow her mom's advice—to be the salmon. To go against the grain.

Now, here she is, filling the shoes of a leader. The brave one. To come up with a plan for them all to escape cruel Banjo's rule.

Even though she's far younger than most of the colony, she refuses to back down. Fear gnaws at her insides, making her voice quiver, but she finally finds her words.

"My dear fellow blue penguins," she begins. "Banjo made you believe that I was being selfish, hoarding loads of anchovies. He turned you against my dad for the same reason."

She motions to Rex next. "But as you can see, Banjo lied about a lot of things. Banjo also made us believe cassowaries were our mortal enemies—that we needed him to protect us."

Rex pipes up. "For the record, I am quite fond of little blue penguins. And I've never once entertained the notion of eating any of you. I'm a vegetarian."

"Vege-what?" someone yells from the crowd.

"Oh, right! Terribly sorry to assume," Rex counters. "I mean I don't eat meat—or any animals for that matter. I'm a vegetarian!"

"What a strange bloke," whispers an older penguin to his graying friend.

Rex recoils in shame and covers his face at the sound of criticism. But then he musters a bit of courage and rebukes, "Hey, aren't you lot pescatarians?"

"Huh? What's he talking about—pescatarians, vegetarians?" the graying friend wonders. "But I kind of like the guy," he finishes with a chuckle and shoulder shrug.

Other penguins chime in, "Me, too!"

A group of teenage penguin girls then proceeds to swoon, calling, "We love you, Rex!" as they try to reach out and touch him with their flippers.

Feeling again like the rock star from his dream, Rex yields the floor to Ripley. She continues: "Thanks for your attention. I agree with you all! Rex is one super special bird. With his encouragement and help yesterday, Pip, Shelby, and I traveled to an interesting place—a few of them. But one was particularly miraculous. It was called a bank."

"A bank?" squeaks Celeste, one nearsighted little blue penguin. "Oh. I've been there before. That's the sloping ground bordering the watercourse that confines a water channel. Perfectly lovely when the water level is normal."

"Sorry, love. Slightly different concept. She means a financial bank," Rex corrects.

"Oh, right. A financial bank. My bad. Carry on," says a blushing Celeste.

Ripley continues. "One hundred and forty-five anchovies, give or take, is not a lot to invest in a bank, by some bankers' standards. But we did learn about lots of cool concepts, for example, savings accounts and certificates of deposit—also called CDs. Given enough time and a decent interest rate or return, we can earn a lot of additional anchovies, a.k.a. money.

"There's this concept of compound interest at the core of lots of investments, which is crazy amazing. But we would need a lot of time to benefit from it, if the interest rate is low." (Sidenote and reminder: Most human kids do have time on their side. We think this is kids' financial superpower.)

The penguin audience listens intently.

"Then we started thinking of a bigger goal—about buying our way out of our contract with Banjo. Unfortunately, to get to at least five thousand anchovies, we can't rely alone on interest from savings accounts and CDs. We would need to get creative and look at other investments. I also don't think I can do it alone."

"Can you explain what interest is, please?" Kai asks, raising his hand.

"Right, sorry, mates. You haven't gotten the same mini-lessons in finance that Pip, Shelby, and I have. Interest is the amount of money a bank will pay you the longer you keep your money with them. You can also earn money with other investments, like stocks," says Ripley. "Isn't that right, Rex?"

He nods at his star pupil. "With stocks, we call the money you make or earn a return. I couldn't have said it better myself. And with compound interest, you earn interest not only on the money you deposit or invest, but on the interest you have already earned as well."

Ripley wants to bask in Rex's compliment. Instead, she's preparing for what she's about to request of her fellow penguins. Her Herculean idea. "As I said, a hundred and forty-five anchovies are not a whole lot, especially for what I'd like us to accomplish. But if we work hard, and if we save our anchovies together, we could invest them in stocks. And if we did well, we could earn enough money to buy our freedom from Banjo."

The colony stares at her blankly. They have no clue what she's saying.

But Rex does. And he can't believe her words. "Just how many anchovies are you trying to raise? I thought we agreed that stock-picking was too risky for the moment."

Ripley clears her throat. "Well, how about twenty-five hundred anchovies?"

"What?"

The little blue penguins' eyes bug out. Indigo faints in surprise.

Still, Ripley doesn't back down. "Come on, everybody. Let's be salmon. Together."

21

A Bunch of Yelling Little Blue Penguins Is No Picnic

Ripley wants to put her flippers over her ears to drown out all the noise. The sound of a hundred energized blue penguins talking—OK, hurling questions at her about her plan is loud and confusing.

"This whole thing is preposterous, if you ask me," says Indigo. "You want to go against Banjo? After all he's done to us? You're asking for trouble."

"Heck. We already *know* he's mean," says Charlie, Shelby's father. "He just ripped out our feathers."

Indigo doesn't back down. "Correction. He ripped out *some* of our feathers. Not all of them. Some of you young'uns haven't been around for as long as us old timers. You don't know the half of how cruel he can be. You have it good!"

At that, more arguments erupt.

Shelby fires back. "*Good?* Just yesterday Banjo branded Nigel's shoulder. And what about Larry?"

"Psssh," Indigo snorts. "That's nothing. Back when I was a whippersnapper like you, Banjo was worse. Much worse. Misbehaving penguins didn't just get a few feathers plucked out. They got picked up by Onyx, flown high up into the air, and dropped to their deaths. Like with Larry, yes, but we witnessed it every day."

"Whoa. That is bad," Pip chimes in.

It's also not entirely true. Indigo made that story up to scare everyone because she's afraid of change and risk. The idea of saving and investing rattles her. Still, it helps that she's seen so much. Fellow penguins don't usually question her motives.

And yet she's not alone in her concerns. Perry piles on the naysayer train. "Banjo isn't just mean. He's ruthless. He'll stop at nothing to get what he wants." He points a flipper at Ripley and Nigel. "You two of all penguins, you should know that. Look at what happened to Sapphire."

"That's my point," says Ripley. "If Banjo can take my mom's life, he can do that to any of us. Or worse. That's why we must work together. That's why we need to buy our way out and put an end to the torture and control."

More arguments break out inside the colony. Rex finds himself smack in the middle of two heated penguins who stab the air with angry flippers.

One wants to follow Ripley. The other does not.

Watching them quarrel, Ripley can't help thinking how crazy it is that the biggest news in modern penguin history—that cassowaries are not scary monsters after all—has been pushed aside. But as we know, fear can be all-consuming, no matter the source. And Banjo remains super scary.

Suddenly, Kai calls for quiet.

He pushes into the center of the arguing match. As the coolest penguin, he's able to harness the colony's attention rather quickly. Ripley waits to hear him talk. Having his support would really help her.

To her relief, the first words out of his mouth make her think he's in her court. "I know I'm on the young side, but Ripley's on to something here. It's past time we revolted against Banjo. But I have another idea."

Ripley feels her stomach sink. Her chances of reaching her penguins seem to be slipping away.

"Investing in stocks sounds risky. How many of you know what the stock market is or how it works?" Kai asks.

Shelby, Pip, and Ripley raise their hands. No one else moves.

"Exactly. It could be a scam for all we know, maybe no wiser than gambling. I'm not a fan of gambling, and I certainly wouldn't ask any of you to give me money to gamble. Let's just work extra hard. Why don't we just double the amount of anchovies we catch every day and save up five thousand anchovies. We can even save them in the bank, if you want."

Rex and Ripley lock eyes. Kai has a point, Ripley thinks, although she hasn't done the calculations herself yet.

"I'll field this one." Rex turns to Kai. "My good penguin, let's apply some math to your suggestion. Who knows how many anchovies you collect per day?"

"I can help you there," says Stuart, the only little blue penguin in spectacles. Obviously, wearing glasses doesn't guarantee that anyone is smart, but in this case, Stuart is very intelligent. "By my calculations, a penguin collects sixteen anchovies a day on average."

Rex pulls out a pencil to draw on the soil beneath his large bird feet. "Thank you. Can you also tell me your daily quota—what Banjo demands of you?"

"Certainly. We must give him ten anchovies per day. Or else."

"Got it, chap. Much obliged." Rex writes down that number, too. "On average, that means each penguin in this charming colony has just six anchovies to live on per day. Do you feel like that's enough?"

Shelby and his dad shake their heads 'no' first. Then the rest of the colony joins in. Stuart speaks up for them. "Mr. Rex, sir, if I may. Living on just six anchovies a day is not very much food for us penguins. Not at all."

"Please, call me Rex," says Rex. "Only my mother calls me Mr. Rex. Now then." He turns to Kai. "Let's test the feasibility of your concept. Could the colony raise five thousand anchovies by doubling the number of fish you catch daily?"

Hearing it put that way, Kai isn't so sure. "Maybe."

Rex does some more math on the ground. "Now, there are a hundred of you lot here. Let's go easy and say you caught an additional six anchovies. Do you think you could catch twenty-two, on average?

"Hmm," says Shelby. "That could be hard. When we fish harder, we're usually hungrier, too. I'm not sure if we could make it on just six daily anchovies."

"And how many of you could imagine catching thirty-two?" Rex continues.

No one raises their hand. Then Nigel slowly puts up a flipper.

"It would seem physically impossible, but I guess we could at least try?" Nigel says, trying to be positive. The thought of being free of Banjo wasn't a prospect he had considered before. He was intrigued.

"No way!" chimes in Leo. "I'd love if we could catch that many, but there's realistically zero chance."

"I would have to imagine you're right, sir. Let's look at it this way: Even if each of you saved an additional six fish daily and consumed no additional fish..." Rex peers at Shelby and mouths an apology.

"Even if you could save another six fish daily, by running yourselves ragged," Rex repeats, "that would take you slightly over eight days. What do you think? Could you survive eight days at that pace?"

"I don't know who you lads are kidding. There's literally no chance we could increase the amount we catch like that. We are already busting our flippers!" Denim contributes.

Ripley speaks up next. "Denim's right. It took me months to save a hundred and fifty anchovies. I was swimming and hunting as well as I could. I know some of you are faster and stronger, but I think at most, we could only fish an extra three on average, on a good day," Ripley explains.

All the little blue penguins hang their heads miserably. They know she's right.

"What is it?" Rex asks.

Stuart agrees next. "No penguin can collect that many anchovies in a day. Nigel was the best, and even he has only ever managed to get twenty."

"And that was on a super lucky day," Nigel adds.

Rex looks perplexed. "But I thought you said *on average* you usually collected sixteen anchovies per day."

"That's on average—spread out among the colony," Stuart explains. "Top penguins like Ripley and Kai help us to get our average up to sixteen per day."

"The rest of us aren't that good," Indigo adds. "Some of us only get ten a day. Or less. The better divers help those who don't catch as much. But no one has saved or started a collection besides Ripley."

Realization dawns on Kai. "So my plan's impossible. Because we'll never catch that many anchovies to possibly pay off Banjo."

Ripley speaks up, softly at first. "It would appear so. And how many of you have had to share your fish with someone else? How many of us are *already* barely getting by?"

Kai turns to Ripley, making her blush. He's never spoken directly to her. She's uneasy with his personal attention. "OK, I'm ready to hear your whole plan."

The colony pivots toward Ripley. She thinks she will collapse under their stares. Heart in her throat, she musters her courage. "OK, everyone. Here goes..."

22

Don't Panic. Buy the (Ranch) Dip

One hundred and ninety-eight little blue penguin eyes are fixed on Ripley. (Double check our math for us, will you, please? If there are a hundred little blue penguins, and each has two eyes, but Ripley can't look at herself, how many little blue penguin peepers must be staring at her at this very moment?)

Thank you. Right then. One hundred and ninety-eight eyeballs fixed on Ripley feel paralyzing. She waits. Maybe she shouldn't want to do anything about Banjo. Perhaps the status quo is the best and safest option. Let life continue as before. She and her family and friends could just continue working for Banjo. Not so bad, right?

That is, until it is bad. Until one of them makes a mistake.

Then Banjo, Onyx, or the Tasmanian devils would punish the little blue penguins, torture them—who knows how. It could be worse, much worse.

It could be...a painful death.

Bottom line: There's no way Ripley could return to her daily routine now. There's no way out...except through.

Ripley knows too much. She and her feathered friends need to swim upstream, against the dark forces working against them.

Hey, Ripley thinks. *That's a good way to explain things*, the idea she's been thinking about since her visit with Hugo at the Koala Bank.

"There's no way to combat Banjo's cruelty," she tells her colony, who waits for her to explain her plan, "unless we act like salmon."

"What in the blazes does that mean?" asks Stuart.

Ripley's left eyelid twitches. This public speaking thing is hard. (No wonder some of you reading this don't like giving book reports in class!) "It means we do the opposite of what most other animals would do. We swim against the current because what we can achieve when we do—when we all swim together—is worth the effort. It's worth the risk."

Rex thinks he knows what she's after and decides to lend her a hand. (OK, maybe he lends her a talon.)

"I believe what Ripley means is that the only way to defeat Banjo is to infiltrate his ranks—to become a spy, if you will. You take down his massive empire from the inside. Isn't that right, Little Blue?"

"What? No. Not at all." Ripley shakes her head vigorously.

"Oh." Rex looks around sheepishly. "Well, that can be plan B, though, can't it?"

"Probably not. I'm not sure it's even possible."

"It's possible all right. You'd simply need an assortment of clever disguises, some convincing makeup, and perhaps a bit of voice acting training."

"Huh?" Shelby asks.

The crowd shifts uneasily. Ripley senses she's losing them. "No, I have a different idea, but thank you for yours, nonetheless."

"Well, 'never say never' is my motto," responds Rex.

Ripley is about to engage with him some more when she sees he's fallen asleep. He's snoring on his feet, in fact, taking one of his unannounced cassnaps.

She turns to face the crowd instead. "Let me break it down. What we need to do, everybody, is pool some extra anchovies."

"Pool anchovies?" Kai asks.

"Yes, until recently, I don't think most of us had considered saving. It was forbidden, and some of us didn't see the point. I propose we each start to save a few extra anchovies and store them in a safe place."

"Save our anchovies?" asks Indigo. "What for? By golly, aren't we done with the risky behaviors?"

Pip jumps in. "Investing."

Ripley is shocked to hear him speak so confidently, let alone in front of the large crowd. He looks toward her for reassurance, and she nods back with a smile. "Go on, Pip."

Bright-eyed with excitement, Pip continues. "We recently learned that investing is a truly magical thing. First, though, you need to save. Then you put that savings in a bank where you can invest it. It's like planting a tree. Investing takes time. But after a while you can end up with something better or bigger. Like a lot more money. Or a huge tree." He points to the magnificent magnolia tree towering over them. Most of the crowd exhales and takes a deep, calming breath.

He gets it, too, Ripley thinks.

"But I like eating anchovies as soon as I catch them. I don't want to wait around to see them grow into a tree," says Shelby's dad, Charlie.

"Meeep! Even so, what's the point of pooling anchovies together anyway? How is that related to investing?" asks Perry. "Our anchovies swim in the ocean, an ocean that has no limits."

"Sincerest apologies," says Rex, awakening from his nap. "Some of these new terms must sound like they belong to a foreign language. Ripley doesn't mean you should move your fish to a pool. In her sense, to 'pool' means to collect them, put them together, SAVE and INVEST together."

"That's right. Thanks, Rex. If we each saved a few extra anchovies, we could use them to buy stock in public companies," Ripley continues. "There's a particularly successful company I have in mind. It's called Daintree, after the Daintree Rainforest, and I think we should buy some of their stock. We should buy some of the company."

Rex listens intently, not sure where she's going with this. After all, hadn't he advised her that Daintree might be too risky of a choice?

"You see, I keep wondering if investing isn't like choosing a good friend." Ripley looks at Shelby, who's not sure what she means either. "It takes time to really get to know a good friend. You spend countless hours together, go on adventures with one another, laugh together, cry together, and occasionally even try to tear each other to pieces. You get a sense of their values, their fundamentals, what makes them tick." She pauses, then smiles. "You know a good friend when you have the good fortune of having one."

A tear comes to Shelby's eye. He thinks of the argument they had before stumbling upon the Koala Café and wishes he had hadn't lost his cool. *How could I be so lucky to have Ripley as a best friend?* he thinks. Ripley is a true-blue friend. (Pun intended!) No matter how goofy and silly he acts, Ripley is always there for him.

Ripley continues. "When you truly know your friend on a fundamental level, would you turn your back on him? Would you throw him to the curb when he began floundering? I don't think any of us would."

The penguins shake their heads to and fro. As they do, a few penguin beaks collide, making clicking and tapping sounds.

Ripley seems to have connected with the penguins on a deeper emotional level. She sees mothers hugging sons, sisters embracing, fathers tussling their daughters' head feathers. Schoolmates playfully punch each other in the shoulders with a wink and then a fist pump.

Ripley continues. "Now imagine you found a company that you knew had a lot of solid qualities, solid fundamentals. Its leaders might make an occasional misstep, or more often perhaps, something happens that is out of the company's control. That event can have a negative effect on the company and its reputation. But. If you truly believed in the value of that company, the way you loved your friend, would you abandon it when everyone else did?"

"Meep!" Perry speaks up. "I'm still confused about stocks and company value, but of course not. I'm not abandoning anyone or anything when the going gets tough. I would stick with my friends, and I suppose with a good company, for the long haul. As long as they're good at their core, I'm all in."

The crowd is surprised by his certainty. You might recall Perry's been known to run from his fears, even ones that are highly unlikely to materialize.

"Well, if my friend lied, cheated, or stole from me, I don't think I'd continue to support her," Denim counters.

Emboldened by the fact that the penguins are engaged and exchanging ideas, Ripley responds. "I'll give you that, Denim. One hundred percent. There are certain behaviors that are inexcusable. We shouldn't let emotion cloud our judgment. But we know a good friend when we've found one, right?"

The crowd cheers, "Right!"

Shelby starts chanting, "Ripley! Ripley! Ripley!" until the crowd catches on.

Ripley beams. This is a lot of pressure for her to shoulder, but her gut tells her she'll be able to steer her fellow penguins well. She smiles and bows before the crowd, silently mouthing a modest, "Thank you." She blows tender kisses to show her gratitude before raising her voice again.

"I believe we have found such a super solid company. Daintree is truly a company worth investing in. It's generally well-run; it's made lots of money for many, many years, and it is a sound business at its core without much competition. But recently, it's suffered a bit of shock. Its share price is down. There was some bad news that made the price sink, in fact. I can't lie to you. It's down a lot. Way down."

Rex nods in agreement and feels his stomach churn again. We think he probably has lost a lot of money on his Daintree investments, too. Hearing Ripley speak reminds him of his predicament.

The penguins listen intently. "On the bright side, this might be a golden opportunity to invest. A few days ago, we couldn't have afforded one of their shares. I have no idea when Daintree's share price will go back up again, but I really think it will. It was tremendously high for many, many years. Lots of animals still want to place orders with them. I hear they make tons of money."

Rex is blown away by Ripley's reasoning. His stomach pains ease. She's even managing to convince him to think of Daintree's stock in a positive light again. "It's undeniable. Daintree is a solid company," Rex contributes.

"Ripley, if you're right, and I think you just might be, you have a truly brilliant plan. What you're suggesting also has a name in the investment community. It's casually called buying the dip. It means you buy stock in good companies when they're 'on sale.' Put differently, you buy the stock when the price is low."

"Did someone say dip? I love ranch dip! Or did you mean French dip, as in the sandwich? Count me in!" exclaims Shelby, ever the jokester. He starts dancing by himself in the crowd. "When I dip, you dip, we dip," he raps quietly, busting a few '90s dance moves.

Ripley and Rex chuckle together. Rex leans down and hugs her from the side. They aren't sure the other little blue penguins understand Shelby's joke, but the crowd's loud, and most probably couldn't hear anyway. Ripley's just happy to have him on her side.

"Aren't there big warehouses being built on the other side of the hill?" Cobalt asks. "Daintree warehouses, I think. You can even see them from here." He points in the distance, and several of the penguins turn to look.

"He's right," admits Indigo.

"I've seen signs for Daintree, too," says Kai. "Isn't that a delivery company or something? I hear they ship things all over the world."

"Yes, indeed!" says Nigel. "Thanks for the reminder. I should order some Mantle Xenoliths from them."

"Some Mantle whats?" Pip asks him in a whisper.

"I'll tell you later, Pip," Nigel says. "I'm putting together some beautiful jewelry for your mother."

Pip smiles. Even his dad seems peppy again, no longer burdened by his aching shoulder, his missing feathers, or just plain worry. He still mourns Pip and Ripley's mom, though.

The prospect of moving their community forward, together, has the whole crowd energized. *Ripley truly has a gift*, Pip thinks.

"If we invest in Daintree's stock when the price is low, we could wait and sell when it's high. The chances of Daintree's stock price increasing are pretty good. I have a good feeling. When it does, we'll end up with more anchovies. Hopefully lots more anchovies—maybe even enough to buy off Banjo."

Ripley beams at the crowd, optimistic that the demise of Banjo's reign might be near. She's also excited to have introduced investing to so many other little blue penguins.

Except they don't all understand.

"What's the stock market?" someone asks.

"What's a stock price?" someone else's sister asks.

"What's Daintree?" that someone else's little brother asks.

"What's an anchovy?" someone else's grandma asks.

Ripley realizes still she has lots to explain. "Imagine you had a huge pumpkin—"

She and Rex take turns breaking down the concepts she's recently learned: value, compound interest, stocks and shares, share price, the stock market. By the end, she's speaking almost as quickly and excitedly as Rex had during their initial adventure to the Piggy Bank.

Finally, she turns to the crowd and asks, "Any questions?"

Ninety-five little penguin flippers fly up in the air. *Oh, no,* she thinks. Maybe she won't be able to explain everything to so many penguins after all. This is going to require some time, more time than she has. How will she ever convince them to join her?

Ripley wipes her now sweaty eyebrow and takes a deep breath. Nothing else comes to mind.

To her surprise, Celeste speaks up. "I don't completely get it. But I like the idea of getting out of our situation with Banjo. And I want to learn more. Maybe we just need to try it out. I'm with Ripley. I want to be a salmon."

Nearby young penguins nod in agreement. "If we save enough anchovies, pool them together, and make a wise investment, maybe (just maybe!) we can free ourselves from Banjo," one of them says. "Finally."

Kai agrees. He smiles at Ripley. "You obviously know a lot about this. We'll follow your lead. How many anchovies does everybody need to save to make this plan work?"

At that, Ripley gulps, unsure how they'll react.

23

The Pact

The rookery stares at Ripley in disbelief. It's so quiet beneath the magnolia tree she can hear a leaf flutter to the ground. Let's be real: Ripley wouldn't mind trading places with that falling leaf right about now. That lucky leaf doesn't have to do anything but exist. No one's pressuring or making demands of it. Oh, to be that peaceful.

Unfortunately, Ripley can't shapeshift into a leaf or trade places with it. Sad, right?

She has just announced how many anchovies each little blue penguin will have to save and contribute for their plan. Judging by their looks, the penguins aren't pleased. They've remembered how worn out and tired they were. Their fleeting excitement has turned to silence. Again.

"That can't be right," says someone finally.

"Say what?" asks someone else.

"You want us to live on *how* many anchovies?"

That last question came from Shelby. *This will be a careful balance*, she thinks.

"The young lady said one." Indigo crosses her flippers. "And we should give her five. She thinks we can all survive by just eating a solitary, stinking anchovy per day. It's madness."

"That's what I thought she said," says Celeste.

"One!" screams Perry. "Meep! It can't be done. We'll all starve to death."

Murmurs of agreement ripple through the crowd. Ripley watches as one after another the waddle's support appears to fade. Even her dad seems to have changed his mind. Nigel avoids eye contact with his daughter, inspecting his feet as if he's seeing them for the first time.

Overwhelmed, Ripley's eyes travel up to the sky then back again. In the night, the magnolia tree appears as a soft, large patch of darkness. Its blurry shape blends gently into the night's silvery glow.

"It's just for a few days. If we just saved five anchovies per day," she begs.

Struggling to decide what to do, Ripley's eyes detect the edges of the tree's broad, waxy leaves. They cast fragmented shadows, rippling slightly in the breeze, creating shifting shadowy patterns on the ground. The magnolia's blossoms, now in full glory, catch and reflect faint moon rays, appearing as pale ghostly orbs.

Kai comes forward, his face scrunched into a look of concern. "Look, Ripley. I really think you're onto something with the whole investing in the stock market thing. It's outside-the-penguin-box thinking, for sure. But, well. You're saying we hand you all the anchovies we don't give to Banjo? That's tough."

"Almost all. Right." Ripley manages to keep her face neutral, so no one can sense the doubt she feels. The night air feels cool on her skin under her feathers, making her shiver—even though she's been much colder than this before.

"I know it sounds hard to do what I suggest. But if everyone could save just five of the anchovies you'd usually eat, I think we could reach our target quickly. Then we invest, wait, and eventually...we buy our freedom."

"Our target?" Stuart asks.

Ripley proceeds patiently. "Yes, the twenty-five hundred we need to buy Daintree stock. I think our best chances of getting to five thousand happens if we can make our investment double. Half of the amount we need to give Banjo for our freedom is twenty-five hundred."

Stuart starts to blink, running the calculations in his head. Those spectacles truly weren't just making him look smart all those years. Of course not. He's downright analytical.

"If we could revisit the whole saving-five-anchovies-a-day thing," says Leo. "Um. That's a lot of anchovies." By coincidence, or perhaps fate, his tummy rumbles.

The sound serves to remind everyone just how much Ripley is asking of them all.

"If we change our behavior for too long, Banjo is more likely to catch on," says Ripley. "I would say we could save a little less each day, but I think that's even riskier. And we can't run to the bank every day to place the anchovies in safe keeping, unfortunately. It's too far."

The crowd continues to listen. "Saving a little each day definitely seems more manageable," Pip agrees. "But we know Onyx and Banjo are watching our every move. They would love to catch us and snatch our hard-earned fish."

"Thanks, Pip. You're exactly right. We must balance a few factors. Since saving isn't allowed under Banjo, we must be extra careful, extra stealthy. It won't be easy," Ripley admits.

Cobalt raises a flipper. "I get it. It's hard work, this business of *saving*, you guys. Isn't that why we haven't all been doing it? It's easier just to enjoy what we have, as soon as we get it."

Curious, everyone turns to look at the young penguin. "Go on," says his mom.

Emboldened, Cobalt continues. "Saving anchovies is challenging. Maybe it's a little like saving someone's life.

You can't just save someone without doing something hard, can you?"

His question prompts a lot of little blue penguin head-scratching. Literally, the entire rookery scratches their heads, eyes darting left and right, as they process Cobalt's words.

"You know what else is hard work?" Cobalt continues. (The little guy is apparently on a roll now.) "Slaving away every day for Banjo."

"Here, here!" says Indigo. "You have a point, Cobalt." She's so proud to witness another of her penguin pupils in his newfound element, taking a leadership role, thinking both critically and collaboratively.

Cobalt smiles at the approval he receives from his mentor and then continues. "At least if we work hard to save our anchovies, we'll have a chance of finally helping ourselves."

"Slay, queen!" hoots Shelby from the other edge of the crowd. "Cobalt knows what's up."

Cobalt chuckles and cheers with his flippers in the air.

Ripley thinks momentum is still building.

But just like that, there's a new comment from the crowd. "If Ripley's plan even works," Perry says, still a mild skeptic. "That's a big *if*."

"Absolutely right, Perry," Ripley concedes, understanding the need to be fully transparent. "There is no *actual* guarantee with this investment. But I have a good feeling about it, a really good feeling. If I'm wrong, we will have worked crazy hard for five days, and then that would be it. I won't ask another thing of any of you. Promise."

Stuart pushes his glasses up on the bridge of his beak, unintentionally making himself look even smarter for his next comment. "Hmmm, I say it's too risky." Ripley is stunned.

"Me, too," says Leo. "Ripley's just a kid, a kid like Shelby. What could she know?"

Ripley locks eyes with Shelby. Her friend just shrugs. *And for good reason*, Ripley thinks. *It's hard to be criticized for being young.* She isn't sure how to respond. She doesn't have a lot of experience with investing. Leo has a point.

"Unfortunately, I'm still out," says Indigo. "Risky business isn't really my cuppa, darling. Terribly sorry to disappoint."

Ripley's heart sinks as one by one, additional little blue penguins reject her plan. They step away and return to their burrows, literally and figuratively distancing themselves from her and her plan. When all is said and done, only two penguins remain by her side.

"I will do this with you," says Cobalt, one of the two. "It's a pact."

"Me, too," says Pip.

They slap flippers in a high five to seal the deal.

Having their support buoys Ripley's hopes, just a little. Yet as she looks around the colony, she sees that they're alone. Even Kai has refused to join them.

Remembering the kind words of encouragement he had shared in front of the whole waddle, Shelby finds renewed courage. "Oh, all right." He winks at Ripley. "Me, three."

Shelby's tummy rumbles loudly, too. "Ignore that, everybody. It's just my stomach saying g'day."

Ripley sighs, a little relieved that she's not taking on everything by herself. But she will have to craft a new plan. Careful not to hint to any potential worry, she promises herself to stay positive and keep going. After all, she still has Cobalt, Pip, and Shelby beside her. "Looks like it's just us. Let's catch some anchovies!"

24

Diving Fever

Monday morning, the little blue penguins trudge from the beach to the sea. OK, *almost* all of them. Ripley, Cobalt, Pip, and Shelby do not plod along like the other beaten-down penguins.

No, these four little ones have pep in their step. Sorry, in their waddle. Ripley especially.

The leader of this mini-crew, she has vowed not to let naysaying penguins discourage her. Even though, if we're being honest, her current plan has no chance. She had needed all ninety-nine of the other penguins to pitch in. All she has are three supporters.

"So what if the others don't like your idea?" Rex says when he finally wakes from his latest cassnap under the magnolia tree. "At least your friends and you are doing something. That's progress!"

He has a point, even if it is a weak one. She and her friends were doing what Sapphire would have recommended.

Ripley and friends were swimming like salmon.

As Ripley speed-waddles to the beach—with purpose—Onyx notices her unusual enthusiasm. Soaring high in the cloudless, southern Australian sky, the seagull spots the energetic quartet. From behind his mirrored aviator sunglasses, his something's-off-but-I-don't-know-what-it-is meter goes off like a smoke alarm in a burning building.

"Something's fishy. What could they be up to?" he mutters to himself.

He swoops to the sand in front of the penguins, just before they reach the ocean.

"What in seven circles of insanity is going on here?" Onyx demands. Slower on land than in the air, he must tread very quickly to keep up.

"What do you mean?" Ripley asks, refusing to slow down. "We're off to the sea to work. To collect anchovies for Banjo."

"Yeah," Shelby adds. "Like we always do. We love our work."

Onyx squints suspiciously at the rest of the colony. Everyone else shambles along slowly. They have their typical awkward, slow gait. And they look as defeated as ever.

Onyx refocuses on the foursome. Standing in stark contrast to the crowd, Ripley, Shelby, Pip, and Cobalt are straight-up jolly. They look excited to be here. They've just hopped into the waves.

The scene still doesn't compute for Onyx. He senses mischief afoot. Again, he questions the crew as he ditches walking to follow them overhead. "Really. You can't fool me. Just what is the big idea here, kids?"

Cobalt answers as he tries to swim past the waves. "No big idea, Mr. Onyx, sir." He plunges under white sea foam, then pops back up. "Honest. We're just happy to be here."

Onyx shoots them another quizzical look. "I don't buy it. Something weird is going on."

But Onyx knows he shouldn't complain about any of the penguins working hard either. One at a time, they plunge after anchovies like they're flying underwater. Back and forth, up and down they soar, snatching anchovies one after another after another. Before noon, they've each caught an average of ten.

Extra verve in her flippers today, Ripley has managed twelve.

She's so intent on figuring out a path to their collective penguin freedom, she loses herself in diving. (Do you know that feeling when you're so deep in thought or enjoying what you're doing so much that nothing else in the world seems to matter? Have you enjoyed reading a super gripping book [like this one!] so much that you didn't realize you had been at it...for hours? Now *that*, our fine feathered or feather-free friends, is what we call flow state.)

Ripley's in her flow state. Every other worry has slipped away from her. She's in a zone. The only thing driving her is this: *scoop up more anchovies*. She does so with gusto.

So, it isn't surprising that Ripley fails to notice that Indigo's been calling her name each time she resurfaces. Again and again. And again.

"Ripley! Ripley." After several unanswered calls, Indigo pulls Ripley aside with a firm tug of her flipper.

Indigo's big eyes flash cautiously. "This has got to stop, young lady."

Her words tear Ripley from her diving trance.

The two of them float near the shoreline as the sea cradles them like a vast, endless blanket. The water ebbs and flows with the rhythm of the waves. Sunlight glimmers on the water's surface, dappling sleek blue feathers with flashes of silver.

"What do you mean?" Ripley asks Indigo, catching her breath.

"You're catching too many anchovies, young lady. It makes the rest of us look bad." Indigo motions to the rest of the colony that dives much more slowly and depressingly.

Ripley hadn't considered the optics.

She only had wanted to catch as many anchovies as possible. And for once, she was enjoying it again. She didn't know what could come next. She hadn't figured that out yet. "I-I didn't realize. Sorry."

"Well, now you know, missy. Please put an end to these shenanigans. You and your whole family have been a real pain in the rear end for us old timers for a long time." Indigo appears crotchetier and more irritable than usual, Ripley thinks. Most of the time she's strict but at least fair.

Ripley's cheeks burn with a mix of anger and embarrassment. She's about to retort when she notices someone else swimming toward them. *Dad.* Ripley had been so focused on making it out to sea this morning, she had forgotten to check on him or say goodbye. Her stomach lurches.

"Ripley!" he calls to her.

Oh, no, she thinks. *Now he's going to scold me, too.*

Ripley braces herself as he draws closer.

"You've been busy," he says, catching his breath. He points to Pip, Shelby, and Cobalt who still haven't stopped diving. "And so have they."

Indigo scoffs. "Busy making us all look bad."

Nigel nods. Ripley's heart sinks. *He's going to tell me to slow down, too.*

"I expected you to fall on your face." Nigel locks eyes with Ripley. "What you said sure sounded like an impossible plan."

"It *is* a crazy plan," Indigo cuts in.

Nigel stares off into the distance, thinking. "But when I watch you young bluejackets effortlessly snagging anchovy after anchovy, it reminds me of something. It reminds me of...well, *being alive.*"

"What?" Ripley and Indigo ask at the same time.

"Heck. It makes me want to catch some anchovies right alongside you. Would that be all right? We were so busy being miserable under Banjo we'd forgotten there's still so much to enjoy."

His words hit Ripley like a wave, lighting up her face with a grin. She can't stop smiling as her father copies her, diving into the sea. Then others from the colony join. Nigel pops back up in front of her.

"So, what I really meant to say was *thank you*. Thank you for helping me find the joy again, chickadee."

Ripley's eyes well up with warm tears. No one has called her that since her mom disappeared. Possibly more importantly, she hasn't seen her dad this happy or genuinely lighthearted in years.

One after another, the penguins swim and dart faster and with more energy than Ripley has witnessed in ages. Their excitement is as contagious as a viral Instagram post. First goes Kai, then Perry, then Stuart, Celeste, and Marin. On and on the list goes. Penguin after penguin floats, dips, and dives in perfect streamline formation, nimbly capturing anchovies. Finally, even previously grumpy Indigo's mood turns, and she joins the raft.

Ripley stares in amazement, her happy eyes now full of joyful tears. *How quickly things have changed, again. For good.* She wishes her mom could be here to witness it. Whether they manage to collect twenty-five hundred anchovies or die trying, Ripley will remember today as the start of something special.

Little does she realize someone else has noticed them from afar.

Banjo.

25

Five Days Later

The little blue penguins do not look great. If you thought they had looked wretched a few days prior, under the magnolia tree and after Banjo's goons had plucked their feathers, you should see them now. (Close your eyes and try to imagine this.)

The first word that pops to mind is *skinny*.

Skinny doesn't accurately describe this unfortunate colony. We need a more pointed word than skinny.

Luckily, we always keep a thesaurus nearby for this very reason.

Let's consult that handy-dandy resource for the right word to describe our little blue penguins' current appearance:

- Scrawny (Check!)
- Gaunt (Good one.)
- Bony (Yep. That, too.)
- Skeletal (Sad. But also, unfortunately, true.)

These are all good adjectives for how the little blue penguins appear, but if we had to suggest just one description, we'd settle on *skin and bones.*

You might be thinking, *Yikes! That's horrible. What happened?* Any guesses?

You also may be saying to yourself, *Wow. This is such a great story, jam-packed with tons of twists and turns, plus seriously funny comedy. It's also taught me so much and gotten me interested in investing and finance!*

Dear reader, thank you for your kind words. They mean a lot. Also, book two will be out soon. You should probably go ahead and reserve your copy.

But back to the whole skin-and-bones ordeal-io. Living on only one anchovy per day—even if that day is sprinkled with joy and excitement—is much tougher than Ripley and the penguins had anticipated.

"I'm dying!" Pip groaned on day four.

"Just. One. More," Celeste chanted to herself, trying to elevate her mood, despite the impossible pain of hunger.

Indigo flopped lifelessly on the sand with weariness on day five.

Even Cobalt fainted as he handed over his last catch to Ripley for temporary 'safe-ish' keeping. (On the evening of day one, Ripley had managed to dig a massive underground cave in her burrow. It isn't as safe as the bank, of course, but it would have to do until they could get their huge stash of twenty-five hundred to the Koala Bank.)

Even though Ripley's dad had gotten the colony excited about pitching in, Nigel had grown weak from snagging so many fish. He's exhausted and wonders if he'll survive. *If I die, at least I will be reunited with my beautiful wife, Sapphire*, he thinks to himself.

The little blue penguins appear so gaunt, we should wonder if any of them will make it.

Perry worries. He tells anyone who'll listen that he's concerned about his sudden and rapid weight loss. "NO one should feel this weak and hungry all the time."

Until day three, Shelby and Charlie had looked lean and strong. That was short-lived though. They quickly passed from looking trim and fit to painfully gaunt, just like the others.

Stuart, the resident bookworm, has started warning the others about the long-term effects of growing too thin. "Did you know your ears could fall off?" (We aren't sure this is possible, but the mind plays crazy tricks when we're exhausted or hungry.)

Even usually upbeat Kai fades fast from lack of food. He tries to block out all thoughts of anchovies to get through this five-day process. But that's tough when you must spend all day diving for anchovies, first for Banjo, then by saving for Ripley's investing idea.

Guess who's not exhausted? Can you think of someone who's not a penguin and who doesn't take cassnaps in this story? Banjo. As you know, he's been watching the penguins with increasing suspicion. At first, he had hoped the penguins had just been working hard to avoid further punishment.

But after a few days and discussions with Onyx, he began to wonder if it could be something else.

"Keep an eye on them," Banjo ordered Onyx. "There's something fishy brewing."

Of course, Onyx did his master's bidding. He spied on the little blue penguins to understand why they would throw themselves into diving with such enthusiasm.

No one would tell him anything.

The little blue penguins kept their collective plan a secret. Not even the little ones, like Pip or Cobalt, divulged their modus operandi. (That's a fancy word for plan.) Every penguin knew the stakes were high.

But Banjo is no dummy. There's zero denying that the penguins were terribly skinny.

Sure, Banjo may be super mean. Sure, he also may have bad morning breath and terrible table manners, but one thing he's truly not? Stupid.

No, he's one crafty dingo.

And so, on the eve of day five, having watched the small penguins waste away, he decides to get involved. Bright and early on day six, as Ripley and friends trudge (once again) to the sea, he steps out of the shadows and confronts them.

"G'day, mates," he says directly to Ripley, an evil grin across his scruffy face. He assumes she must be the motivator of whatever mischief has been transpiring.

Ripley stops, far too exhausted to flee. Pip and Shelby stand beside her.

Ripley's blood runs cold. She doesn't like Banjo's expression. Nor can she sense any warmth from the Tasmanian devils that flank him like an offensive line in football, guarding their quarterback. Of course, she wouldn't expect any different. Still, Ripley never likes seeing Banjo or any of his henchmen.

"H-hi," says Ripley slowly, not knowing how to respond, barely able to function from exhaustion. As far as we know, extreme hunger won't make your ears fall off. But it will make your brain work slowly. Very slowly.

An inability to think is the last thing Ripley needs right now. Not when she's face to face with the cruelest villain down under.

"Looking a bit thin there, aren't we?" Banjo points to Ripley's emaciated frame.

Ripley ransacks her brain for some excuse, something reasonable to explain her state. "Oh," is the only she thing she can muster.

Banjo points to the other little blue penguins. "You're *all* looking rather gaunt. Very thin. And the last of your feathers—they're falling out."

None of the colony dares respond to Banjo.

Instead, they stare blankly ahead of themselves, their eyes glazed over and bleary. They're too fatigued to come up with a believable lie, too weak to even care.

"What I find really interesting," Banjo continues as he peers into Ripley's eyes, "is that all of you have been working hard. *Really hard.* But where are all those anchovies you've been catching?"

The rookery slowly turns toward Ripley, awaiting her answer.

This is a lot of pressure for a kid. But she's practically used to it by now. Plus, she's so exhausted and depleted from the past few days that she feels more numb than nervous.

"Explain yourself," Banjo demands.

"Uh..." Ripley can't think of anything else.

"*Uh* is not an answer, little girl."

"Well..." Her brain still can't function. She blinks as if in slow motion.

Banjo narrows his eyes, baring sharp teeth. "Neither is *well*."

Ripley feels weak. A high-pitched ringing starts in her head and gets louder. A cold sweat forms on her forehead.

Banjo reaches into his trouser pocket to remove an anchovy. He dangles it in front of her. "Eat this."

Ripley shakes her head, her beak pursed firmly shut—even though she's literally dying of hunger.

"Eat it. And then you and I are going to talk. *Alone*."

The whole colony, plus Banjo's minions, stare as the evil overlord forces the anchovy onto Ripley's skinny flipper. "Eat it," I said.

Ripley wants nothing more than to eat the juicy, delicious morsel. She wants it so badly she can practically taste its delicious saltiness on her tongue.

But she knows it wouldn't be fair to eat one before everyone else. Her fellow penguins have been starving, too—starving because of her plan.

Be the salmon, she thinks to herself.

"EAT!" commands Banjo.

Ripley resists and shakes her head. A hot, sour taste travels from her stomach to her mouth. The acidity makes her burp.

Banjo is livid, his eyes popping out of his skull. *"Why do you continue to disrespect me?"*

But before Ripley can respond, she wilts to the floor. Everything goes black.

26

The Dingo Den

This is just a guess, but you've probably never been inside a dingo's den before. Are we right? Good. Wise choice.

Since you haven't, imagine this: If you were to enter a dingo's den, your poor nose would be attacked by the sharp tang of half-eaten kangaroos. Next, that funky smell would mix with the sickly-sweet whiff of decaying papaya. Dingo dens also tend to be small and cramped. You might not even fit. And of course...they're filled with dingoes who are best to be avoided at all costs.

Unfortunately, Ripley has the misfortune of being in such a den now. Only Banjo's den isn't completely typical either. Why would it be? After all, he's not a typical dingo.

His home is neither small nor dingy. It's spacious and luxurious. Just beneath its surface, underground tunnels slink this way and that. Oil paintings of Banjo himself line the tall walls, his various poses and glowering expressions illuminated by fancy low lights.

But Ripley hasn't seen these yet.

Nor has she been able to peek at Banjo's eccentric butterfly collection. (In between torturing little blue penguins, this rich, megalomaniacal ringleader makes time to capture rare insects.)

Ruthless as he is, Banjo clips off their beautiful wings, while the butterflies are still alive. He then displays them in mason jars, which he bedazzles with diamonds and rubies. Again, this is not your average dingo or den.

Still semi-unconscious, Ripley lies on her back. Her eyelids move slowly. They feel heavy. Once she finally opens them, she screams.

"AHHHHH!"

We think you'd scream, too, if the first thing you saw when you awoke from a traumatic experience was Banjo's face. At this moment, he's chewing the end of a cigar. He wears a burgundy robe made of velvet, tied neatly around his waist. He taps the thick gold ring around his pinky finger on a crystal glass. *Piiing, piiing, piiing,* like the rhythmic chime of a grandfather clock.

Banjo grins slyly at Ripley.

"W-where am I?" Ripley looks around, taking in her unfamiliar surroundings. She tries to sit up but can't muster the strength.

"Welcome to my lair," Banjo chuckles. "I like to call it the Colossal Cavern."

Ripley can feel her slow heartbeat pulsating in her ears. She tries to piece together what must have happened. The last thing she can recall is being confronted by Banjo. She was on her way to work, she remembers. Banjo had been trying to uncover her plan. To coax her to talk, he had offered her an anchovy. Delicious as it looked, starving as she felt, Ripley remembers refusing it.

And then? Darkness.

"You passed out," Banjo cuts into her thoughts. "My guess? You're weak from hunger."

Ripley remains mute. She keeps her gaze downcast.

Banjo grabs her under the base of her beak, forcing her to look up at him. "Come now, darling. I brought you here for a reason."

Ripley glances around the room with a deep gasp.

It's the most elegant place she's been. It's even more ornately decorated than the Piggy Bank. She feasts her eyes on stunning marble statues and crystal vases. Ornate pillars span from floor to ceiling. There's even an enchanting waterfall overflowing with what appears to be liquid gold. Or perhaps it's platinum.

"Like what you see?" Banjo grins smugly. "This is what being rich, rich with anchovies, can buy you."

Ripley tries to avoid looking at the seafood buffet that is being arranged on a long table to her right. It's covered with delectable seahorses, shrimp, and scallops—treats she would love to devour, especially in her famished state.

"Are you *absolutely* sure you wouldn't like anything to eat? My treat." He pauses. "Dearie?"

Ripley's tummy betrays with her with a loud rumble.

Still, she shakes her head. She's worried, though. *What might Banjo do if I continue to reject his offers?*

The canine scoundrel chews the end of his cigar more aggressively as he paces the floor of his den. "You know, I get so tired of being a brute all the time. It's *painful* for me to have to punish you. It's *boring* to pluck out feathers. In fact, I simply detest violence; don't you?"

"Y-yes, sir." Ripley tries unsuccessfully to keep the quiver out of her voice.

"It's utterly *uncivilized*." Banjo points to the bounty of luxury that surrounds them. "I'm a gentleman first. A businessman second. A lot of animals don't realize that."

"Yes, sir," Ripley replies, unsure where Banjo is headed with his comments.

"And as a gentleman and a businessman, I want to see my anchovies continue to pour in. But that only happens, if I have good penguin workers."

Ripley tries to hide the disgust she feels for him. "Yes, sir."

"But you, little girl, appear bent on jeopardizing all of that. There's something about you. Some rebellious streak. It reminds me of your mother."

Inside, Ripley is screaming at Banjo. Still, she keeps her cool. "Yes, sir."

"The other penguins. They look up to you. Don't they?" Banjo knows the answer to his own question.

"Yes, sir."

Banjo stops pacing. "I see something in you, too. You're a natural leader. And natural leaders deserve to be rewarded for their smarts. For their bravery. How would you and your dad and brother like to have a nice, fancy burrow like this one day?"

Ripley can't believe her ears. *"Excuse me?"*

"I could have my T-devils build one for you. You know Bork, right? Well. Your home—we could construct one large enough for your friends, too."

Ripley struggles to process his words. "You'd do that? For me?"

"Sure! And that's not all. You, Nigel, Pip, and that portly penguin—what's his name again?"

"Shelby."

"Yes, the big guy. All of you would have additional privileges. You wouldn't have to dive for anchovies anymore.

You could oversee my operations for part of the day and enjoy some leisure in the afternoon."

Ripley knows there must be a catch. "But what about the others?"

"They would have to work, of course. The anchovies must keep coming in, after all. I would be willing to do all this for you, Ripley, on one additional condition. You must tell me what's really been going on with the colony."

There it was. Finally.

Ripley understands his approach. Bribery. He's only pretending to be kind, the con artist.

"So, what do you say? Would you tell me what's really going on? If you do, I promise to make everyone you love very rich. None of you will ever have to work again."

Ripley's stomach aches. She stares at the buffet table longingly. She pictures her dad taking it easy. He could be healthier, happier maybe. Pip would have a great life, too. Shelby and she could enjoy themselves, starting now.

But at what cost? Ripley would doom the rest of the colony. The ultimate betrayal. *How could I do that to them, after all we have been through together? What would the salmon do?* she wonders.

Ripley clears her throat. "I wish I could help, but there's truly nothing going on, sir."

Banjo picks up a chiseled vase and hurls it at the wall, making Ripley jump. Porcelain shards scatter in all directions.

"Foolish girl! You have just made a terrible mistake. Starting tomorrow, you have yourself a new quota. I'm increasing everyone's daily catch count by three. You lot will bring them in, or else."

27

Desperation, Penguin Is Thy Name

That night the whole colony converges at Ripley's doorstep. They still look haggard and painfully skinny. As you would imagine, they haven't eaten enough to regain their strength, let alone their ability to think clearly. How do you feel when you're hungry? Maybe a little hangry? Well, guess what. The same thing happens to penguins. They're currently *very* hangry.

Hangry at Ripley.

Perry confronts Ripley. "You traitor. You're working for Banjo now, aren't you?"

"What?" Ripley can't believe her ears. That's the worst accusation a fellow penguin could have hurled at her. Her thin feathers stand on end much like you and I get goose bumps. She looks like a cross between a scared porcupine and a panicked penguin, in fact.

"Easy. Easy." Kai pleads for calm. "Before we start getting crazy, Ripley, you should know that there's a rumor circulating that Banjo plans to make you one of his new deputies—"

"Did you sell us out? After all we did for you," Indigo questions.

Ripley tries to contain the growing shock and panic inside her. She must defend herself, but she still can't think straight. The optics of her meeting with Banjo weren't good. But before she can say anything, Pip pushes through the mob to her side. "You leave my sister alone. She would never work for Banjo. Never. And you know it."

A new, thinner version of Shelby comes running up behind Pip. "That's right. Ripley loves us unconditionally. She's the most loyal penguin I know." He pauses to whisper, "You are, aren't you?"

Pip pinches Shelby's stubby tail. "Of course, she is. That's my sister you're talking about."

"Then why was Ripley gone so long at Banjo's den? What were you doing there, hmmm?" Denim inquires.

"We know that answer," says Charlie. He had once been three times Ripley's size. Now he's so scrawny he looks like he traded his oversized blue tuxedo for a slim-fitting suit. Beyond that, his feathers continue to fall out. "I bet she was taking bribes from the big man. I just know it. She's in line to be the next Onyx. She and her dad. You just wait and see."

Ripley knows the little blue penguins aren't thinking straight, but she's sad to be losing their trust, nonetheless.

Nigel's eyes go wide. "Is there something you're not telling us, Rip?"

A hush falls over the crowd as they await her answer.

Ripley's beak trembles. "There *is* something I have to tell you, Dad. Something I was working up the courage to say after Banjo cornered me in his den."

"I knew it," says Perry.

"Hush." Nigel bends over so he's at Ripley's eye level. "Well, what is it, sweetheart? You can tell me anything."

"There's something I have to tell all of you, actually." Ripley takes a deep breath, steadying herself. "Banjo did offer me a leadership role."

The entire colony gasps audibly. Ripley worries they might attract Onyx's attention. "Shh, please quiet down. I absolutely turned him down!" she insists.

"That's my girl!" cheers Nigel as quietly as possible while still celebrating. The rest of the penguins aren't ready to let Ripley off the hook, though. They frown at her.

"How can we believe that?" asks Perry.

"Well, unfortunately, when I turned him down, Banjo got a little upset. He just increased our quota. Starting tomorrow, we owe him three extra anchovies, per day."

"No!"

Gasps fill the air. Perry panics and runs up and down in place. Indigo faints. Some of the parents shield their eyes so their little ones can't see them cry. Nigel falls back on his bottom in despair.

Only Kai retains the power of speech. "B-but that's impossible. We cannot possibly catch that many fish. We're barely hanging on now. We haven't even recovered."

Nigel tries to keep the concern out of his voice. "That can't be."

Ripley hangs her head, finally defeated. "It is."

More sobs erupt from the crowd.

Suddenly filled with energy, Indigo picks herself out of the sand. Eyes blazing, she points an angry flipper at Ripley. "Look at the mess we're in, all due to your meddling in things you know nothing about."

Stuart shakes a fist at her. So does Charlie. "You silly penguin. Always wanting to do things differently."

Perry piles on next. "Silly is right. We were doing just fine until you showed up with all your 'bright ideas.'"

Saddest of all, even Kai turns on her. "I should've seen this coming.

You're just a kid. What do you know?"

They're right! Ripley thinks. *Maybe they would have been fine working for Banjo. Maybe it wasn't the best life, but it was easier than their current situation.* She's too worn out to discuss anything.

"I'm so sorry," she says through tears. "I truly am. From the bottom of my heart."

Perry jumps into the fray. "No more listening to Ripley."

"Hear, hear," says Indigo. "About time you spoke some sense."

They're not alone. One by one, all the older little blue penguins turn on Ripley. Again. In seconds they form a circle around her, Pip, Shelby, and Cobalt.

Pip locks eyes with Ripley. "What do we do?"

"There's nothing for you *to* do," says Kai. "The old mentality is back in charge again."

Shelby scoffs. "You're not much older than us."

Kai ignores him. "Forget this investing business. We're taking back all those anchovies we saved."

Thunderous applause meets his suggestion.

"At least we'll have some food in our stomachs, when we go back to working for Banjo," says Charlie.

"Agreed," says Indigo. "How I look forward to eating those fish we caught!"

"Me, too," says Charlie hungrily. "We'll have a big feast. We'll chow down on all those tasty anchovies we've been piling up."

"Yum. I can already taste 'em," Shelby adds, his mood brightened.

Pip pinches him again. "Whose side are you on?"

"The food's side." Then he looks at Ripley and changes his mind. "Kidding. Kidding!"

Kai breaks through the group, heading straight for Ripley's burrow.

Nigel stops him. "Where do you think you're going?"

"Step aside. We know Ripley's stashed all the anchovies here. Those are our anchovies. We'll be taking them back now, thank you very much."

Even if Nigel had wanted to stop Kai, dozens more little blue penguins have lined up behind him. They have also flanked him on either side. There's no escape.

Seemingly conquered, Nigel turns sadly to Ripley. "I guess we have no choice, my dear. Give them what they want. At least you tried. We all did."

Nigel lets them pass before Ripley can utter a word.

There's a scream inside the burrow so loud it shakes the home's thick, sandy walls.

"EEEEKKKKK! Where. Are. Our. Anchovies?!" shouts Kai through gritted teeth.

Pip and Shelby look surprised. "What do you mean?" they ask.

Rex appears out of the blue, behind a pack of penguins. "I can answer that. I deposited them in an account at the

Koala Bank for you. For safekeeping. Not to worry, it's all according to plan."

Indigo looks like she might have a heart attack. *"You did WHAT?"*

Unruffled, Rex, politely proceeds, "I can take a few of you with Ripley and me tomorrow afternoon. To the Koala Bank. How does that sound?"

28

Back to the Koala Bank

The little blue penguins waddle down Wallaby Street toward the Koala Bank.

Hugo is behind the desk, and he's busy today.

That makes perfect sense. If you recall, since koalas sleep most of their lives, they must be super careful how they allocate their time. This is especially true when they work at a bank that is only open for twenty minutes a day.

So, when Hugo looks up to see Ripley, Indigo, Perry, and Kai, he knows he must get straight to brass tacks. He's a little intimidated to see Rex back so soon, too.

"Ugh. You lot again?" he says, cleaning what looks like minty green eucalyptus juice from his tie. He must've forgotten to clean up after his shift as a bartender.

Kai observes his surroundings with awe. "So, this is a bank."

Hugo smiles politely at the chap. "Yes, indeed. We're always pleased to welcome new clients."

"Let me introduce you to Hugo," Ripley tells Kai. "He also works as a marvelous bartender."

"Side hustle?" Indigo puffs herself up in her wicker chair, so she can look taller. "I'll take one of those and a splash of eucalyptus juice, please. Wish I had time for that," Indigo scoffs. "All of us had to dive for anchovies this morning on empty stomachs. You ever tried that, Mr. Hugo?"

"Can't say that I have. Then again, I'm not a bloody little blue penguin. So, if that's all you came in to tell me, thank you for your visit today, ma'am. I'm happy to show you the door—"

"Pardon her, please. She's running low on rest and food these days. Could use a little R&R, if you know what I mean." Rex gestures for Hugo to sit down. "We have important business with you."

"What business?"

"I'll tell you what business," says Perry. "You're sitting on top of our hard-earned anchovies. Now give them back, you scoundrel."

Hugo exchanges another look with Rex. "Is this one mad, too?"

Sidenote: In Australia, it's quite common to call someone "mad" instead of saying they're crazy. Although in this case, Perry is also mad about the colony's anchovies being locked away in the Koala Bank's vault.

Kai echoes Perry's pleas. "Please, Mr. Hugo. I think there's been some mistake. This little girl here—"

"Stop calling me a little girl," Ripley interjects.

"Excuse me. *Ripley* mistakenly gave you the anchovies our rookery worked so hard to save."

Hugo holds up his paws as though he's about to be arrested. "No, she didn't."

"She didn't?" asks Indigo. "So, she *was* lying. I knew you were a traitor."

"You didn't let me finish," Hugo continues. "Rex gave the bank your colony's anchovies. He and Ripley are customers of our branch now. They earned a free toaster just for opening a brokerage account. Isn't that lovely?"

"What the blazes is a toaster?" asks Perry.

Hugo's face lights up. Perhaps toasters are his fourth passion, after banking and bartending and quilting, of course. "Toasters are marvelous inventions. You can use them to heat all kinds of leavened bread items. But since I only eat eucalyptus leaves, I haven't much use for them. I like toasters more in theory."

Ripley checks the clock on the wall. They have exactly twelve minutes until closing. They need to pick up the pace.

Fortunately, Kai is also in a hurry. "That's great about the toasters. What we want to know is can we please have our anchovies back?"

Hugo turns to Ripley for confirmation. *"All of them?"*

Ripley nods sadly.

Hugo looks confused. "But I thought you had big plans. Weren't you going to use your money to invest in an amazing company and then win your freedom—or something similarly noble?"

Ripley wishes Hugo would stop talking. She wishes all of them would stop talking. It's bad enough she had to come here again, this time with Indigo, Kai, and Perry. Now she must listen as they dash her dreams, their dreams for all of their futures.

But Hugo isn't done talking. He's on a roll now. "Because, folks, I have interesting news for you. It's about Daintree."

Ripley snaps to attention. "What about Daintree?"

"Its stock price has gone down again. To $100 a share."

Perry smacks the table with his flipper. "Didn't I tell you we shouldn't get involved? You hear that? The stock price went down. Again. Where's the bottom?"

Rex chuckles. "In our case, that's a good thing, mate."

"It is?"

"A very good thing," Rex says. "I did some additional research, and I see next to no chance Daintree's stock won't skyrocket again soon. That's my humble opinion, of course. I could always be wrong, but I have a good feeling. We just happen to be able to buy it for a little less than we initially expected. My only question is, why did the stock price go down further, Hugo?"

Hugo shrugs. "Demand is high, but Daintree can't fill orders, particularly for certain food items, it turns out. So, a few more large investors have decided to reduce the number of shares they own—their holdings."

"Even the piggies?" Ripley asks.

"I'm not sure about the piggies," Hugo responds. "But I think it's a problem Daintree will be able to fix. They've faced issues like this in the past and worked through them quickly."

"Who cares about piggies?" Indigo is undeniably grouchy. "We're not investing, Ripley. Now give us our anchovies back, Sir Koala, or whatever your name is. I've got to get back to my burrow before nightfall."

Ripley is lost in thought, her mind working overtime. Finally, she turns to Rex. "A hundred dollars a share is significantly lower than it was the last time we were here."

"Yes, it was trading at $250 only a week ago. We had based our calculations on those stock prices."

"Who cares?" asks Indigo. "Now, Mr. Koala, if you please—"

"Hugo, ma'am."

"Fine. *Hugo.* Can we have our anchovies back?"

"It's up to Ripley. She and Rex are my ultimate customers. They're the ones who got the free toaster for opening an account, if you recall."

Kai, Perry, and Indigo stare at Ripley expectantly.

"Tell him to release the anchovies," says Kai, tension in his voice.

"Yeah. We want off this ride, kid," Perry adds.

Hugo addresses Ripley. "Do you want all twenty-five hundred of your anchovies back? It's your call."

Ripley's tummy rumbles. It's like a gas tank running on empty. She's so hungry she can barely think. But she must. Her colony's survival depends on this.

"Can I have a minute?" she asks.

Kai groans. Perry rolls his eyes. Indigo looks like she'll scream. "We don't have a minute."

"Actually," says Hugo. "You have six minutes until closing time."

Ripley excuses herself. What a relief to step outside of Hugo's office with all those extra penguin pressures. She wanders into the lobby and nearly runs right into Banjo—of all animals.

"Pardon me," she says automatically.

By a stroke of luck, Banjo didn't notice her. His face remains hidden behind a stack of papers, one of which says Blue Futures.

Ripley rushes back into Hugo's office.

"Banjo's out there." Ripley pants.

"What? How?" says Indigo.

"We're goners," says Perry.

"He'll see us if we try to cart out twenty-five hundred anchovies," says Kai.

"Then let's not," says Ripley. "Maybe this is a sign."

"It's not a bloody sign," says Indigo. "We just have to come back tomorrow."

"Can't," says Hugo. "Bank holiday."

"Fine," says Kai. "Then we'll come back the next day."

"'Fraid not," says Hugo. "That's the weekend. We're closed then."

Rex locks eyes with Ripley. "This is your moment. What'll it be?"

Some inner strength fills her at that moment. Even her hunger doesn't bother her. She feels...well, strong. It must be the adrenaline. And she's hopeful, like she used to feel when her mom was still around. She looks at the clock. She only has four minutes left to plead her case.

"I need you to trust me, just this one last time," she tells the other little blue penguins.

Indigo snorts. "How?"

Ripley keeps going. "I didn't trust Rex at first. He was scary and there were all these terrible stories about him. But you learn to trust other animals based on their behavior, their actions."

Kai puts his flipper on her shoulder. "That's all very nice. But we need to get going—before Banjo sees us."

Ripley stays focused. "Rex taught me something. There are times in life when you must take risks—"

"We did take a risk," says Perry. "And look how it turned out."

"Yes," says Ripley. "Look how it turned out. Would you ever believe our colony could have saved up twenty-five hundred anchovies? That's literally half the number of anchovies we need to buy our freedom."

Kai nods. "That is true."

"Would you take all that money back knowing you'd just have to slave away for Banjo for the rest of your life? Today, we owe him thirteen anchovies a day. Tomorrow? It could be fifteen. Or twenty."

Indigo's face relaxes. She and Perry consider Ripley's words.

"Or would you rather take a risk on yourself? I know I am asking you to place your trust in me again, but what if investing is the only way things can finally get better?"

Hugo points to the clock. "You have one minute left."

"Time's running out," Rex tells the little blue penguins. "Will you buy Daintree's stock, or do you want your anchovies back?"

29

An Unexpected Visit

Days later, Hugo shows up unannounced to the burrow. What he sees shocks him. The skinny little blue penguins move slowly. They appear more like prisoners than workers. Almost no one says a word, and they swim blank-faced through the water. They also have even fewer feathers than before. Most are down to just two.

But that's not what catches the koala's immediate attention. Instead, he's surprised to see beasts of burden, camels, in fact, traipsing across the sand with boxes on their humps.

The boxes have the logo "Blue Futures" stamped on them.

That's odd. *What does that mean?* you may be wondering. It's probably something important. We'll come back to that in a moment.

We got you covered. Promise.

For now, allow us to point out a few other oddities. Onyx and the Tasmanian devils are directing the camels who carry the heavy boxes. What are they up to?

Something additional you should know about koalas is this: They don't like the sea. Don't believe us? The next time you go to the beach, look around. We bet you won't see a single koala surfing. Or even sunbathing. It's not their thing.

So, Hugo is probably the last koala you'd expect to wade into the ocean's waves, let alone in today's beige linen suit. But he does.

"Where's Ripley?" he calls out to Nigel and Pip—to any little blue penguin who might hear.

It takes a few minutes of shouting for Celeste to finally point Hugo in Ripley's direction. When she does, Hugo is nearly fully submerged and looking uncomfortable. "Oooh. Salt water is certainly not my cuppa tea."

Still, he's determined to find his customer.

"Hugo?" Ripley asks, coming up for air. "What are you doing here?"

The sight of Hugo completely out of his element, in a drenched, tailored suit, lights up her face and makes her chuckle.

His presence draws the curiosity of more nearby penguins. In seconds, Pip, Shelby, Cobalt, and Nigel have drawn closer, forming a ring around Ripley.

At first, Hugo's expression is hard to read. He looks solemn. Angry—although that could be due to the fact he's getting pelted in the face by waves. And he's sopping wet.

"What is it?" frightfully skinny little blue penguins ask each other. "Who is that, and why is a furry animal in the water?"

"As you recall, I was initially surprised you had only wanted to invest in a single stock, in Daintree..." Hugo begins.

"Yes," Ripley confirms.

"And recall that you had wanted to invest in that company when things weren't going well at all. I didn't think it was a good idea. Didn't like it one bit."

"Yes."

"And almost no one else wanted to touch the stock. In fact, the most seasoned and wealthy of institutions and investors were selling their shares. Remember?"

"Yes," responds Ripley again, more sheepishly than the last time, her stomach now in knots.

More little blue penguins gather around Ripley and Hugo. Worry fills their gaunt faces. They knew the risk. Indigo explained it to them, when she came back from the bank: "We're going to trust in ourselves, one last time," the mature penguin had said, surprising them all. "If we don't risk it now, we'll be servants forever. This is our best shot."

All the saliva in Ripley's mouth has evaporated. Still, she forces herself to ask the question they're dying to know. "Did you come here to tell us bad news? We appreciate your wanting to let us know face-to-face. That's noble." She gazes into the distance, expecting the other penguins to come down on her again. Hard.

"So, did we lose all those anchovies we invested?" Ripley asks specifically.

A hush falls over the colony as they await Hugo's answer.

"I-I..." Hugo's voice trails off. He exhales slowly, choking on salt water.

"What is it, man?" Nigel yells. "Spit it out already."

"I'm trying! I am also just dumbfounded. I can't believe what's happened."

"WHAT?" Pip asks. "Please just tell us."

"There's another company that announced a huge partnership with Daintree. Investors are back. Stronger than before. Everyone's buying a bunch of shares."

"Penguinish, please," says Stuart, who's left his glasses on the beach for the day. "We didn't all go to a fancy finance school like you."

"Actually, I went to bartending school," corrects Hugo.

Ripley forces herself to stay calm. "Please, Hugo. What are you trying to say? What happened to our shares?"

"Investors were so excited by Daintree's partnership with Blue Futures, that the stock price has skyrocketed in the past week. In fact, it's jumped to $400 per share."

Stuart smacks his head with his flipper. "We're doomed!"

"No," says Ripley. "That's a *good* thing. An *amazing* thing!"

"It is?" asks Stuart. "I really should've gone to banking school—or bartending school."

"You still can. But for now, no need, pal. Some basic math skills should do the trick," Hugo offers Stuart. Then he turns back to Ripley.

"And this week," Hugo continues. "Today. Daintree's stock price continues to soar. It's currently $500 per share."

"Is that a good thing, too?" asks Stuart. "Honestly, I'm lost here."

A huge smile lights up Hugo's face. It's the first time he's shown such elation in years. "It's a great thing. Your starting investment of $2,500 is now worth...$10,000."

Gasps all around. Then suddenly—

All the little blue penguins hoot and clap in delight, splashing the waves with their flippers as they hug each other and dance about.

"We're rich!" Indigo shrieks. "Rich!" She hugs the first penguin she sees, who happens to be Pip. She whirls him around as she laughs happily. Nigel high fives Kai. Kai high fives Cobalt, which leads to a high five frenzy. Everyone gets into it.

Only Ripley stands apart. She's speechless.

On the one hand, she's delighted. She wants to celebrate with the others. But she's seen enough bad things in her young life to know not to keep her hopes up for too long. She doesn't want to be let down.

"Hugo," she says quietly. "That company Blue Futures. I saw Banjo at the bank with some papers. I saw that name on them. And I saw someone with a bag and that logo a while back at the Piggy Bank, too. The partnership with Daintree you talked about—is that a partnership with Banjo?"

Hugo turns to look at the camels on the beach. He puts two and two together. "Perhaps. Yes, I suppose it could be Banjo's company."

Ripley is suddenly reminded of the dingo den. Banjo had told her that he was a businessman, and she never knew what he did with all the anchovies they caught for him. He must be up to something. *But what exactly?*

"So," says Hugo. "What do you want to do now? Invest some more?"

"No," says Ripley. "At least not now. Can we get five thousand of those anchovies to pay off Banjo? Let's leave the rest invested, and we can come by next week to talk about other options."

"Smart girl," replies Hugo. "I think we should diversify your investments a bit. Let's look at index funds and some bonds potentially. I also still recommend keeping a little in a savings account."

"Deal," says Ripley. "Can't wait."

"Ahem." Shelby clears his throat. "Don't you think you're forgetting something?"

"What?"

"We're starving. Literally starving. How about we take out another thousand anchovies from our winnings and have ourselves a feast?"

"Good idea," says Ripley.

The colony cheers again. It's so loud, Hugo has to put his wet, furry paws over his ears.

"The only small negative is that there is a portion you will owe in taxes, but you still have enough for your freedom, your feast, and future investments." Hugo pauses and inhales deeply. "For now, just enjoy."

Ripley throws her arms around Hugo. He hugs her back. "Proud of you, Little Blue," he says. "Mind if I call you that, too?"

"As you wish, Hugo. Thanks for making it possible."

30

Wheelbarrows of Fish

Several hours later...

Ripley and the colony watch as a now-dry Hugo returns with two wheelbarrows, overflowing with anchovies. Panting, he can barely push them. They are piled high with six thousand anchovies, wrapped in banana leaves, of course.

"You know, personal delivery is not something I usually do for customers," Hugo tells Ripley. "You're lucky I like you, Little Blue." He nudges her shoulder.

At that second, Rex zooms over at warp speed to give Hugo a dirty look.

"*Fine.* I came here because Rex said if I didn't, he'd eat me."

"Little does Hugo know I'm a vegetarian," Rex whispers to Ripley.

Ripley can't hold back her laughter.

"So," says Hugo. "What do you want to do with these anchovies—"

The nearby little blue penguins don't let him finish his question. Starving, they leap onto a wheelbarrow and begin stuffing their beaks.

"Yum. It IS even better when we don't puke first," says Shelby.

"I don't know," says Charlie. "I kind of miss the puking."

Ripley smiles at Shelby. She's just as famished. But she takes only a single anchovy for herself. She's must keep her wits for what's to happen next. "Rex, it's time."

Rex nods, remembering their plan to regain freedom from Banjo in exchange for five thousand anchovies. He's about to go with her—but then, he falls asleep on his feet. Surprised? We didn't think so.

Not wanting to disturb her friend, Ripley waits for the colony to stuff themselves. She's happy to see her dad smiling as he chows down beside Pip.

"Attention, everyone," says Ripley at last. "Our moment has come."

The rookery feels it, too, and they stand at attention.

"Ready when you are," says Indigo, holding her flipper to her forehead, in salute.

Kai grabs ahold of the other wheelbarrow packed with five thousand anchovies. Nigel and Perry help him push it. The whole colony marches down the beach toward Banjo's den. The little blue penguins look a lot like they did in Chapter 1, when we first met them. Only this time? They don't trudge like hopeless wretches. Instead, they hold their little blue penguin heads high.

At the water's edge they find Onyx, Bork, and more Tasmanian devils.

Onyx's cruel eyes observe the anchovies with shock, then suspicion.

"That's a lot of fishies, boss," whispers Bork.

"Can it!" Onyx tells him. "Where on earth did you get all those?" he asks Ripley.

She shakes her head. "We're here to talk to Banjo. And Banjo only."

Bork makes a raspberry sound. Ripley ignores him.

"Banjo's busy," Onyx says finally.

"But I'll take those anchovies off you," Bork says. "Hand them over."

Ripley knows better than to give Banjo's baddy anything. "We wish to see Banjo—"

"What's all the commotion?" Banjo finally asks, perched on top of a camel. When he sees the bounty of anchovies, each wrapped neatly in a banana leaf, his jaw nearly falls out of his skull.

"What…is this?"

"Our payoff, if you please," says Ripley. "Five thousand anchovies equal our freedom. You spelled it out on the sign over there."

"Is that what that thing says?" says Bork. "I can't read."

Banjo can't stop staring greedily at all the anchovies before him. He practically has money signs over his eyes. For the first time anyone can remember, he's dumbfounded. He doesn't know what to do either. (It's not exactly a good look for Australia's premiere super villain, is it? Even the Tasmanian devils look uncomfortable.)

Out of sheer nervousness Bork burps.

"Boss?" Onyx finally says. "If those penguins don't work for you anymore, who's going to retrieve the anchovies we promised to…?" He stops short before finishing his sentence.

Something odd happens to Banjo's face. Something bizarre. It contorts uncomfortably. He twitches. But he quickly regains composure. He tries to slide down gracefully from his camel. Except something weirder happens. He slips and falls on his dingo face. Now even more uncomfortable, Bork burps again.

"Will you quit that?" Banjo yells.

Unhinged, he starts to pace. He shakes his head frantically with a shudder and a grunt. But his paws are unsteady under him. If it's possible, he looks...well, he looks terrified. It only lasts a second.

Then he gets ahold of himself again. "You did well, my penguin friends. I'm quite impressed. If you can bring in this many fish, we can really make a fortune. Together, of course. *As partners.*"

"Partners?" Indigo explodes. "We're done with you."

"Forever," says Ripley quietly.

"You're done with me?" Banjo says more to himself than to the others. "What am I going to do? You can't leave me. I love you all so..."

Banjo's eyes change. They flash pure evil. He takes a running leap at Ripley. But before he can catch her, Rex intercepts him in mid-air. He gently but firmly places Banjo on the ground. "The penguins are free. A deal is a deal."

"Where'd you come from?" Banjo asks. "I thought you agreed to stay away."

Ripley shoots the cassowary a look. *Rex never told me he knew Banjo.*

Before she can ask about their deal, Onyx slides over to Banjo. He tries to keep his voice down, but Ripley overhears him. "Without the penguins doing our work, we'll be out of business."

A spark of brilliance lights up Banjo's face. "Call down the other seagulls."

"But why, boss?"

"Do it."

Onyx does as he's told. He doesn't see Banjo whisper to Bork a secret order. But Ripley does. She wonders what it could mean. She doesn't have long to wonder.

Within seconds, seagulls descend from the sky. The second they land, Bork and the Tasmanian devils pounce on them, shackling handcuffs around their orange, webbed feet, so they can't fly off.

"Sorry, old friend," Banjo tells Onyx as he handcuffs the seagull himself. "Business is business. Looks like I found my new day laborers."

Onyx stares at his old boss with venom in his eyes.

31

Oh, How the Tides Have Turned

It really is a beautiful sight to encounter happy little blue penguins. We apologize. You haven't gotten to enjoy seeing these flightless birds in their full glory. Throughout these pages, our colony has been frequently miserable, slaving away. Starving. Terrified. Branded and plucked. Nearly falling off cliffs. More feathers falling out.

It's been a real mess, we admit.

But that's not the way little blue penguins usually go about their lives. Normally, they're happy creatures, swimming in the ocean. Eating anchovies. Basking on sun-dappled beaches. Updating their cute social media profiles. Wait. That last one isn't right. Sorry about that.

Anyway, if you were suddenly to be transported to the continent of Australia, you'd be amazed to see Ripley's colony now. For one, they're no longer dying of hunger. That's a big plus, right? Maybe not for Shelby, though. He and his dad kind of went overboard on the whole stuffing your face thing. Honestly, they're so plump that they asked Hugo to keep his wheelbarrow.

They now use it to transport themselves up and down the beach.

The point is, life is finally good for the colony. Really good. You can tell things are sweet because their little blue penguin feathers have returned, giving them all shiny blue, beautiful coats. Also, there's no more trudging to jobs they hate. Instead, their new routines are probably a lot like yours on Saturday mornings. They wake up, yawn, and then decide what fun they can have with their day, free from the burdens of Banjo's torture.

As for Ripley?

Far from being the occasional target she was but a few weeks ago, Ripley is now the rookery's undeniable hero. Even grown-ups like Indigo and Perry regularly seek her advice. She spends much of her days deep in philosophical conversations with Rex, poring over various companies' earnings reports and generally being curious about the world around her.

But what makes Ripley happiest is how much better her dad feels. He no longer mopes around the burrow, mourning the loss of Ripley's mom. Instead, he's found new hobbies like teaching Pip new things. What do you think Pip might be interested in?

If you said platypuses, yes! Congratulations! You finally guessed correctly! Maybe that'll be the subject of our next book. Maybe.

Of course, not everyone is joyous in these parts. There's one group of animals that is absolutely miserable. Can you think of which one?

If you guessed duck-billed platypuses, you'd be off. Those unique beings are still content doing whatever it is platypuses do. No, we're talking about the seagulls.

You see, Banjo is the type of villain who doesn't give a hoot about his minions. That rascally bandit doesn't care whom he must hurt to get what he wants. He even betrayed his own lieutenant, Onyx, and the other seagulls, as soon as Rex made him uphold the contract and free the little blue penguins. We never did find out the deal between Rex and Banjo, but there's something there—you can be sure of it.

Sorry, we got ahead of our skis there. Back to the whole seagull situation. When we come back to our story, the first thing we see is Banjo, that rapscallion of a dingo. He's not actually working. Instead, Ripley notices he's living high on the hog.

That's an apt metaphor because Ripley notices that her old enemy has befriended the greedy piggy banker she once encountered at the Piggy Bank. Ever the curious little blue penguin, she watches their every move from the beach. Banjo is busy hosting a massive party on his yacht, several hundred yards from the shore. Champagne corks fly, and loud reggaeton beats fill the air.

Yes, dingoes can have yachts. Rich ones do anyway. They love them, especially Banjo who happens to be smoking cigars and partying with the piggies. Ripley is not alone as she watches their revelry from the shore. Pip and Shelby stand beside her as well.

"Look at those bozos. I almost feel sorry for Onyx." Shelby points to the sea. A bunch of Tasmanian devils led by Bork are busy monitoring the seagulls as they attempt to catch their anchovy quotas for Banjo. Every few minutes, Onyx and the other seagulls nosedive into the water. But they aren't nearly as productive as the little blue penguins had been.

"I don't feel bad," says Pip. "If you ask me, they got what they deserved."

A piece of Ripley's heart does go out to the seagulls, though. She pities poor Onyx. *No one should ever be abused, not even the meanies.*

Her thoughts are interrupted when something green registers out of the corner of her eye. She turns to see someone familiar. It's the very same crocodiles she saw guarding the Koala Bank weeks ago. Now they're treading toward the water. The whole colony watches in shock as the dark green and brown prehistoric creatures descend toward the waves, wearing tiny police uniforms. Gray fins stealthily poke out of the ocean next, and Ripley notices sharks circling Banjo's yacht.

One particularly large shark, with a bulging chest, leaps aboard Banjo's yacht, a gun drawn against one of his pectoral fins.

"Banjo the Bad," he says in a surprisingly low baritone voice. "You have the right to remain silent. Anything you say..." the shark continues reciting the animal version of Miranda rights as he reaches for something in his pocket.

Empowered by a handy pair of binoculars, Ripley can see the details of the commotion very clearly. (Please don't ask us how she miraculously found these, but do believe us. She managed to locate them just in the nick of time.)

When she sees the shark officer lock cuffs around a seriously mangy pair of wrists, she gasps.

It's all coming back to her. Banjo was at the Piggy Bank that first time she visited. It was *he* who looked familiar, but whom she couldn't fully identify.

"You are under arrest for illegal insider trading." She hears the officer thunder. Banjo looks to Onyx winging low above the waves. "We have reason to believe that you have profited from a recent set of transactions involving Daintree stock—quite enormously, in fact. If convicted, you could face up to twenty years in prison and fines of up to $5 million...per violation."

The other sharks and crocodiles swarm the well-fed piggy bankers who have tried to save themselves by jumping off the yacht. "Not so fast. We'll need to take you all in for questioning as well."

Ever the villain until the bitter end, Banjo simply puffs on his cigar, his wrists bound behind his back. "I demand to speak with my lawyer."

"We'll see about that," says the arresting shark officer. (Incidentally, he goes by the super ironic name of Harry. *Why is it ironic?* We challenge you to find a single hair on his tooth-like denticles (a.k.a. skin).

More sharks and crocodiles close in on Banjo, the piggies, and the Tasmanian devils. Each suspected criminal gets dragged away in handcuffs. As Banjo struts across the beach to the police van, he saves one last remark for Ripley. "This isn't over, young lady."

"Oh, yes, it is," says Harry. Then, he shoves Banjo inside and slides the van door shut.

Ripley cannot believe her eyes. *What just happened?*

In all the ruckus, she fails to notice that the seagulls have been set free. Onyx swoops down by her side. "Something for you," he says.

"For me?"

When Ripley opens the letter, her heart nearly stops. It's her mother's handwriting. The first line reads: "*My dearest chickadee. I am so proud of you. You're an amazing girl and the quintessential salmon."*

"My mom?" Ripley gasps inaudibly. "She's alive?"

THE END

32
Glossary

Term

Investopedia definition (unless otherwise specified)

Ripley's Definition

Asset

Assets are things that have value. An asset may produce income, now or in the future. An asset may appreciate in value over time.

Ripley's Definition: You might think these are a bad word, but they are NOT. They're just things that have value—things you can buy and sell—e.g. some tasty anchovies or a pair of cool sneakers even.

Bank

A bank is a financial institution that provides services such as accepting deposits, making loans, and offering products like savings accounts and Certificates of Deposit (CDs).

Ripley's Definition: This is a special place that protects money, anchovies, and other valuable goods. Two common ways to deposit money in a bank are through savings accounts and Certificates of Deposit (CD). It's also a place to borrow money. Many banks offer additional way to invest money, i.e. in stocks.

Brokerage Account

A brokerage account is an investment account held at a licensed brokerage firm. A brokerage account allows one to invest in publicly traded assets such as stocks, bonds, mutual funds, ETFs, and derivatives. Full-service firms charge either a flat fee based on the size of the account or commissions for the trades that they execute. Online brokerages charge lower fees and may suit investors who wish to conduct their own research, trades, and other account transactions.

Ripley's Definition: This is a type of account used to invest in stocks, index funds, and mutual funds. Brokerage accounts may offer more financial options beyond this as well.

Certificate of Deposit (CD)

A certificate of deposit is a type of savings account that pays a fixed interest rate on your deposit for a set period of time (the term), in return for leaving the money in the account untouched for that term length. The best CD rates may be higher than those of the best traditional savings accounts, but you lose withdrawal flexibility—if you withdraw your CD funds early, you'll typically be charged a penalty fee.

Ripley's Definition: Do you remember this concept from the book? This was the second option Hugo the Koala banker offered us. I could have bought a certificate of deposit, and the bank would have guaranteed me a rate for a certain time. But if I had wanted to use that money sooner, I would have paid a penalty.

Compound Interest

Compound interest is interest on a loan or deposit added to the previous balance, which in turn increases the interest paid in the following period. Compound interest means earning interest on both your original principal and accumulated interest over time, i.e., "interest on interest". Compounding multiplies savings or debt at an accelerated rate.

Ripley's Definition: This is pure magic. You can earn interest not only on the amount you deposited but on the interest you have already earned, too!

Deposit

A deposit is money added to a bank account, for safekeeping or to earn interest. It can also refer to a partial payment to secure goods or services, such as a security deposit on a rental property.

Ripley's Definition: To deposit is to place something (in our case money or anchovies) somewhere—like a bank.

Diversify

Creating a portfolio that mixes a wide variety of investments in an attempt to reduce portfolio risk.

Ripley's Definition: If you diversity, you spread out your risk rather than invest only in one or very few things.

Federal Deposit Insurance Corporation (FDIC)

The Federal Deposit Insurance Corp. (FDIC) is an independent federal agency insuring deposits in U.S. banks and thrifts in the event of bank failures. The FDIC insures deposits up to $250,000 per depositor, as long as the institution is a member firm. The FDIC covers checking and savings accounts, certificates of deposit (CDs) money market accounts, IRAs, revocable and irrevocable trust accounts, and employee benefit plans. Mutual funds, annuities, life insurance policies, stocks, and bonds aren't covered by the FDIC.

Ripley's Definition: We didn't technically have an FDIC in our book. The Little Blue Penguin Finance version was called the Koala Deposit Insurance Corporation. It's a government agency that would guarantee you would not lose a certain amount of anchovies (or money) that you had either deposited in certain accounts at specific banks.

Future Value

Future value (FV) is used to estimate the worth of a current asset at a future date based on an assumed growth rate.

Ripley's Definition: This is the amount we think something will be worth in the future. I thought Daintree would be worth more, after we bought our shares. Was I right?

Index Funds

Index funds mirror the performance of benchmarks like the S&P 500 and other market indexes by mimicking their makeup. Index funds invest in the same assets using the same weights as the target index, typically stocks or bonds. Index funds provide broad market exposure and diversification across various sectors and asset classes.

Ripley's Definition: Imagine owning tiny slices (shares) of all the companies that are traded in a specific market index—a huge collection of public companies across a sector (portion) of the economy. In the US, a two well-known indexes are the S&P500 or the NASDAQ.

Inflation

Inflation is a gradual loss of purchasing power that is reflected in a broad rise in prices for goods and services over time. High inflation means that prices are increasing quickly, while low inflation means that prices are growing more slowly.

Ripley's Definition: Here's an example of inflation—five anchovies might buy me a burger, fries, and a drink today. We're betting five anchovies won't get us as much in ten years—maybe just a drink and fries. That's inflation. It means what my money can buy today will not get me as much in the future.

Interest

Interest is the charge for borrowing money. Interest expense or revenue is often expressed as a dollar amount, while the interest rate used to calculate interest is typically described as an annual percentage rate (APR). It's also the amount of money a lender or financial institution receives for lending out money.

Ripley's Definition: Don't let the Investopedia definition confuse you. When we deposit money in a savings account, we're essentially loaning the bank our money. They pay us for that money because they invest it elsewhere. In exchange, they pay us 'interest.' Similarly, if we borrow money from the bank, we will owe them interest.

Investment

An investment involves using capital in the present to increase an asset's value over time. Investments may include bonds, stocks, real estate, or alternative investments. Investments can be diversified to reduce risk, though this may reduce the amount of earning potential.

Ripley's Definition: This is an active choice to expose your savings to potential growth. There is also a risk of losing some of it, as we have discussed. An investment can have positive or negative returns.

Investor

Investors use different financial instruments to earn a rate of return to accomplish financial goals and objectives. Investors are not a uniform bunch. They have varying risk tolerances, capital, styles, preferences, and time frames. For instance, some investors may prefer very low-risk investments that will lead to conservative gains, such as certificates of deposits and certain bond products.

Other investors, however, are more inclined to take on additional risk in an attempt to make a larger profit. These investors might invest in currencies, emerging markets, or stocks, all while dealing with a rollercoaster of different factors on a daily basis.

Ripley's Definition: I, along with my little blue penguin friends, decided to buy shares of a company called Daintree. We 'invested' in that company. I think you should consider investing, too, but start small!

Mutual Funds

A mutual fund is a financial vehicle in which shareholders put their money together to invest in securities (e.g., stocks, bonds, money market instruments). A fund manager chooses the best investments, and every investor shares in the profits if the investments do well.

Ripley's Definition: I haven't dealt with these yet, but they're a collection of investments in different companies. Managers (people or programs) decide how much to keep invested in each of the companies inside a mutual fund.

Personal Finance

Personal finance is about meeting your financial goals and understanding all the routes to do this, from saving and investing, and keeping debt under control, to buying a home to planning for retirement—and coming up with a plan to accomplish these goals.It's also the name of the industry that provides financial products to meet these goals.

Ripley's Definition: Personal finance is the reason for this book! I hope you can learn and discuss with friends or family what you can do with money—earn, save, spend, or invest it. This is a collection of choices around money.

Portfolio

A portfolio is a collection of financial investments such as stocks, bonds, commodities, cash. You might choose to hold and manage your portfolio yourself or you may allow a money manager, financial advisor, or another finance professional to manage your portfolio for you.

Ripley's Definition: This is a big mix of investments that make up everything someone owns.

Private Company

A private company is a privately owned business that does not trade its shares on public exchanges and is not subject to the same regulatory requirements as public companies.

Ripley's Definition: This is a company that is not listed on a public exchange. You can still invest in these, but the money you invest would be more directly delivered. Another hint: These companies don't get fancy tickers.

Public Company

A company whose ownership is divided into shares that can be traded by the general public. A public company is required to disclose its financial and business information regularly to the public.

Ripley's Definition: This is a company that is listed on a public exchange. These companies share financial information with the public and hope to have people and institutions around the world loan them money i.e., invest.

Rate of Return

A rate of return (RoR) indicates how much an investment's value has changed over time relative to what it cost. The effects of inflation are not taken into consideration in the simple rate of return calculation. In the real rate of return calculation, however, they are. Rate of return=[(Current value–Initial value)/Initial value]×100

Ripley's Definition: The rate of return that we got on our Daintree investment was amazing and not completely likely but also not unheard-of. We made a lot of money...I mean anchovies.

Return

A return is the gain or loss that an investment generates over time. It can be expressed nominally as the change in dollar value of an investment.

Ripley's Definition: This is the amount of money we gained over during the time we had invested. We also could have lost some or all, though, remember?

Risk/Reward Ratio

The risk/reward ratio helps investors gauge the potential return on an investment for each dollar risked, allowing for more informed decision-making.

Ripley's Definition: Typically, the riskier and investment, the larger the potential gain or loss. When other investors thought it would be too risky to invest in Daintree, we made our move.

Savings

Savings is the cash an individual has left after subtracting expenses. It represents a surplus of funds for an individual or household after all the bills have been paid. Savings can be grown through investments and a dedicated savings plan.

Ripley's Definition: Remember my anchovy stash? This was the bundle of anchovies I caught but didn't give to Banjo and chose not to eat.

Savings Account

A savings account is an account at a bank or credit union that is designed to hold your money. Savings accounts typically pay a modest interest rate, but they are considered safe for parking cash that you want available for short-term needs. You'll typically earn a lower rate in savings accounts versus other options like CDs or bonds.

Ripley's Definition: A savings account will help keep your money safe and earn you some interest, but it probably won't be a ton. But, you also can't really lose the money you put into a savings account. Well, that is true, unless someone is able to steal it or you spend it.

Share

Shares are units of ownership in a company that investors can purchase. The terms "shares" and "stocks" are often used interchangeably; however, they are technically distinct. "Stock" is the financial instrument a company issues, and a "share" is a single instance of that financial instrument.

Ripley's Definition: This is a small piece of a company that is yours when you invest in that company. It allows you literally to own a piece of that company. But remember: You can't take it home with you.

Share/Stock Price

This is what you pay for a share of a company. It's the cost for a share of a company's stock.

Ripley's Definition: This price is determined by a market, i.e. a huge number of buyers and sellers.

Stock

Stocks refer to the general financial instruments issued by a corporation, while shares are specific units of that stock that can be bought and sold by investors.

Ripley's Definition: Basically, this is what you want, if you invest in a company. You can also buy company bonds (debt), but that's another topic for another day.

The Rule of 72

The Rule of 72 (or 72 ÷ interest rate) helps estimate how long it takes for money to double under compounding.

Ripley hasn't explored this concept much yet, but she could soon. In the meantime, we thought other little blue penguins and readers might be curious about it. Here's an example: If Ripley invested 100 anchovies into a savings account with 4% interest, it would take her 18 years to get to 200 anchovies (~72/4). This isn't the most precise way of calculating when an investment will double, but it's a good guideline.

Time Value of Money

The time value of money (TVM) [...] is a core financial principle that states that money today is worth more than the same amount in the future.

Ripley's Definition: Here's an example: ten anchovies today will buy you more than ten anchovies in the future. But, if you can invest that money, and the amount of money you earn in interest or investment returns is larger than inflation, you will have lots more money to buy more things, in the future.

Time Value of Money Formula

$FV = PV(1+ni)n \times t$; **where:** FV=Future value of money; PV=Present value of money; i=Interest rate; n=Number of compounding periods per year; t=Number of years

Value

Value is the monetary, material, or assessed worth of an asset, good, or service. The time value of money doesn't account for losses in capital or negative interest rates. TVM uses the concept of the power of compound interest. The TVM formula accounts for the amount invested, the rate of return, and the time frame.

Ripley's Definition: This just means what something is worth. Different people (or penguins) might value things differently.

Withdraw

A withdrawal occurs when money is removed from a financial account, such as a pension, savings plan, bank, or trust.

Ripley's Definition: To withdraw means to take money out of an account.

Made in the USA
Coppell, TX
25 April 2026

76044951R00173